THE COMPLETE
STANDARD POODLE

Eileen Geeson

Howell Book House

HOWELL BOOK HOUSE
A Simon & Schuster / Macmillan Company
1633 Broadway
New York, NY 10019

MACMILLAN is a registered trademark of Macmillan, Inc.

Library of Congress Cataloging-in-Publication Data

Geeson, Eileen.
    The complete standard poodle / Peter Newman.
      p. cm.
    ISBN 0–87605–602–8
    1. Standard poodle. I. Title
SF429.P85G44 1998
636.72'8--dc21   97–46119
                                       CIP

Manufactured in Singapore

10 9 8 7 6 5 4 3 2 1

CONTENTS

This book is dedicated to my husband, Roy, for taking so patiently to a life dominated by my passion for Standard Poodles – and to the memory of Jane.

ACKNOWLEDGEMENTS

Special thanks to top journalist Rod Tyler for his kindness and help in tracking down John Suter and his team of sled dogs in Alaska, and to American photographer Gerry Davies for sending me photographs of sled dogs.

I am indebted to Emily Cain for information on working dogs in the USA and Canada; to Bob and Wendy Ratcliffe for information and photographs of Agility dogs in England; to Dr Elaine Robinson, Molly Windebank and Ann Penfold for American kennel profiles, and to Margareta Salstrom for help with the Scandinavian kennels. Thanks to Anne Beswick and Ann Coppage for historical photographs; to the committee of the Standard Poodle Club for their support, to Viv Rainsbury for her excellent line drawings that illustrate the Breed Standard, and to all those lovely people who sent information about their kennels and supplied so many wonderful photographs.

Finally, thanks to Johnnie and Connie Speight for giving me my first great love – Jane.

INTRODUCTION

Standard Poodles are a special breed, cherished by many people the world over. These dogs are extremely friendly, fun-loving and charming. They are very sweet, kind and tender. They are sensitive and easily hurt, but take what is dished out to them with very little complaint. Laugh and your Standard Poodle will laugh with you. Cry, and he or she will hang their head in dejection and

Standard Poodles are a special breed with a kind, loving temperament.

sadness. They hate you to be upset, but are devastated if you are upset with them, when they may have done something you consider wrong. They love to curl up on your lap, or as near to you as possible, touching you whenever they can with their soft face. A well-loved Standard Poodle will more than match that love in return. It will adore its family, both human and canine. It will be faithful and devoted. It is wise and dignified, with a temperament that is regal.

I do not pretend to know everything there is to know about the Standard Poodle. I would consider it arrogant to think otherwise. However, I have owned them for thirty-odd years, and I have bred a few Champions and some very lovely pets, I have worked in Obedience and played at Agility, I am honoured to be accredited as a Championship Show Judge, and have written about the breed from time to time. I have served as a member of the Standard Poodle Club for twenty years, as East Anglia Area Representative. I love Standard Poodles. I am eternally grateful to the English writer Johnny Speight, who created the hit British television series *'Till Death Us Do Part*, and to his wife Connie, for giving me my first Standard Poodle, Jane, in 1964. Jane changed the course of my life and showed me there was a love and goodness in the world which I never knew existed. Standard Poodles will, indeed, be with me – 'till death us do part!

ATTITUDE TO TRAINING

The Standard Poodle is very co-operative, outgoing and easy to train – a dog that is so quick to learn that it will train you to do its bidding before you know it. Standard Poodles will enjoy training classes but understand that this is where their owners learn to train their dogs, and Standard Poodles go to have a few laughs. The cartoon character Snoopy depicts the Poodle well when he states of his owner: 'He already does everything I want him to, why do we need training classes?' Attend a training class and watch the owner who throws the dumbbell, only to go and retrieve it himself – now, that is a well-trained owner. Love your Standard Poodle to bits, but do train him, or you will not be the master. Train him well and you probably still will not be his master, for he will think for himself and object to doing things he considers stupid and no fun. Co-operate he will, when he can see the sense in so doing.

Standard Poodles are addictive. I hardly know anybody who, once having owned one, changes to another breed. It is far more usual for owners to get a second Standard Poodle. Two are better than one. Two are great fun together – and you do not need to feel so guilty about going out and leaving them, when they have company. I know many pet owners who started with one Standard Poodle and now have two, three, and four. So be warned!

THE PROTECTIVE POODLE

In times of trouble the Standard Poodle will protect his owner. They do make excellent

Janavons Barry Sheene on the motorbike ridden by Barry Sheene when he won the World Championship. Once you have owned a Standard Poodle, you will be content with no other breed.

Photo: Eastern Daily Press.

house dogs, guarding your property, and making a lot of noise when strangers approach. Many a perfectly behaved, demure and well-mannered Standard Poodle can suddenly turn into a teeth-snarling wild beast when faced with something which really challenges his post. In the book *Travels With Charley : In Search Of America* by John Steinbeck we are told how John's Standard Poodle Charley, the gentlest creature, and seemingly most cowardly on earth, suddenly tries to defend his owner from a huge mountain bear.

Standard Poodles have an in-built, inherent, intuitive awareness. Sometimes they will take in a person with a distant sniff and ignore them completely, or back away and grumble under their breath. When such a friendly dog does this, who knows what they are seeing through? If you find yourself with a shy Standard Poodle (which is a different case altogether from the outgoing, friendly dog who has an instinctively clever brain and backs off from danger signals) then you must socialise him more, but not allow people to force their attention upon him. He will come round, given time and patience.

THE THOUGHT-READING POODLE

Standard Poodles are intelligent beyond measure. They read thoughts. Do not ever doubt that before you have hardly hatched a plan, your Poodle will know about it. Think about going for a walk later – and your Standard Poodle will pester you until you do. Think about bathing the dog – and it suddenly disappears. If it happens to be one of those Standard poodles that rather like the bath water, and there are many that do, you will find it jumping in the bath almost before you have reached the bathroom!

Standard Poodles are marvellous alarm clocks. Many times I have gone to bed thinking that I must wake up at a certain time. Minutes before the alarm clock rings, one or two of my Standard Poodles will nudge me awake and mooch about until I get up. They, of course, then get into my vacant warm spot. The same applies if I do not set the alarm – which dispels any thought that the dogs somehow get a signal from the clock that the alarm is shortly to sound.

If you think about not being sure whether you like a certain person, on meeting that person your Standard Poodle will look sceptical, and may even refuse to be touched by them. One of my most friendly of bitches, Cha Cha, would not go near a particular man who attended my ring training classes. I could not understand this at all, because she loves men and I knew this chap was a nice guy. It suddenly came to me what was happening. He smoked a pipe, which I hate. Unconsciously I was silently protesting my disapproval and Cha Cha was picking up these unapproachable vibes from me. Once I realised what was happening I did my best to be more sympathetic in my attitude towards the pipe habit, and hey presto! Cha Cha decided the chap was not so bad after all. She went up to him of her own accord and allowed him to pat her.

Standard Poodles are extremely susceptible to their owner's mood. They are impressionable and readily touched with emotion. If you are going through a bad patch in life, with family arguments, then quite expect your Standard Poodle to react by doing something out of character; something you will misapprehend and class as naughty.

This susceptibility will work both ways. Think about impressing a new acquaintance with your clever Poodle and it will more than likely have the last laugh. Think about going out and leaving your Standard Poodle on its own and it will hang its head in sadness, or curl up in its bed sighing, or follow you about like a clinging child,

The Standard Poodle is a breed of immense intelligence and perception.

attempting to make you feel guilty about leaving to have fun while it is positively neglected. On your return you are greeted with such enthusiasm it is sometimes difficult to get through the front door past the avalanche of overwhelming Standard Poodle trying to get you with its enthusiastic tongue.

I have owned and worked with many breeds of dog and found some to be highly intelligent, but I am convinced the Standard Poodle is different. More like a human. Having said that, it is as well to remember that a dog is a dog and not a human substitute. Self-centred, so-called dog lovers heap their inadequate, frustrated lives on to the back of the dog. They heap imaginary kindness upon the dog, denying it any of its natural desires, sometimes inflicting a form of cruelty in an effort to satisfy their own inadequacy. They feed a dog tidbits until it is so fat it looks ready to burst. They refuse it any natural raw food and bones because they do not fancy it; preferring to feed the dog treats and sweet biscuits, and nothing more than that dreadful muesli-like food. The dog ends up fat and neurotic.

This is a breed that thrives on human companionship

USING BODY LANGUAGE
It is said that Standard Poodles understand every word one says. To speak to an uneducated dog is like trying to converse with a foreigner, who probably is only capable of understanding 'yes' and 'no' in our tongue because we happen to nod or shake our heads unconsciously when we speak. Standard Poodles, I am convinced, quickly learn to understand more than the average dog, and they speak back to you if you will only listen.

Say to you Standard Poodle, "My, you do look posh," and it will prance about with a nonchalant air, stepping high on its small oval feet, tail carried high, head tossed back like a model on a pedestal, its almond-shaped eyes full of sparkle. Say to your Standard Poodle, "I think we will go for a walk" and it will wag its tail and probably its whole body, circle you with excitement, or bark with great enthusiasm. Sign language, or body language, can be easily learned.

Your Standard Poodle wants something from you. "How about taking me for a walk?" He nudges you under the arm for attention, walks over to the drawer where the lead is kept, proceeds to the door, then back to you. He may be saying, "I liked that dinner you gave me tonight." Rubs face on carpet, bottom in air, tail high and wagging, sometimes makes loud grunting noises. He is telling you, "I like you." Nudging, rubbing his body against your legs, washing your ears and your face if he can get at it. "I am not amused with you." Curls up, sighing, casting sneaky, suspicious

Keeping two Standard Poodles is twice the fun!

glances your way. "I'm hungry." Is a thorough pest, pawing you, belting the newspaper you are trying to read with his paw, picks up dish and carries it about in his mouth, or bangs it with feet, lays head in dish with a sigh as last resort.

You ask your Standard Poodle a question. He is not sure of the answer – wags tail slowly from left to right. He knows the answer undoubtedly – two full wags from side to side, look of dignified importance upon his face. Ask your Standard Poodle if he fancies a tasty dish of egg, bacon, sausage and beans, or a dog-dish of dried dog-muesli. Watch the different reaction. The response is rather like the one you get from a child when it is asked if it wants fries or green vegetables.

Watching your Standard Poodle is time-consuming but very worthwhile. You will become fascinated on realising how much it has learned just by watching you. Unless your Standard Poodle is an extremely rare specimen, its bad habits and undesirable traits can be laid at your door.

THE GREGARIOUS POODLE
The Standard Poodle does have a clever insight into our personalities which gives it a distinct advantage. Standard Poodles love human companionship as much as they love each other. They do not take readily to being excluded or being alone for any length of time. If you do not want your dog to be part of the family unit, then do not buy a Standard Poodle. It will make demands on you, if it is denied proper attention. If you love it to bits and take care to look after its daily needs, which are not much after all, it will repay you by being

obedient, loving and loyal. If you mean to go out to work all day and leave the dog alone, do not buy a Standard Poodle puppy, no matter how desperately you think you need one. It will feel dreadfully lonely, aggrieved and insecure, and start to alleviate its frustration, usually on your valuables.

If you must go to work for more than a few hours a day and you must have a Standard Poodle, then the best solution is to have two. They will occupy each other and, normally, never get into the habit of destruction. I say normally, because when puppies are at play they can knock things over and tug at loose ends. Remember to be tidy and leave them somewhere safe. Never, however, leave puppies if you cannot get home at lunchtime to break their day, have a game of ball in the garden or walk them. Good owners get up that extra bit early and walk their dogs before leaving them. Also leave them with good meaty raw bones to chew. It is also important to take care that your Standard Poodle has plenty of space when you leave it or them. Unless my dogs are messy from their walk, I leave them the freedom of the whole house when I go out. When they come back from a splash and rough and tumble over the nature reserve they are lucky enough to run in daily, then I leave them

with bones to chew in the utility room. Dogs are fairly claustrophobic and will react with some sort of neurosis when they are constantly being shut away in a small room.

Think very seriously before taking on a puppy. Maybe the time is not right for you. Be honest. It is better to wait a little longer for that puppy than to have to part with it to a rescue shelter when you find you just cannot cope – which is usually heart-breaking for both of you.

Standard Poodles are happiest when they are with you. They love to ride in the car with you and will sit happily in a car waiting for you to take them for a ride. It is a good idea to introduce your puppy to the car from a very early age, taking it out at every opportunity. Do not leave your dog in a parked car with the doors shut, even in mildly warm weather. Shut yourself in an enclosed car for ten minutes with the sun beating down on it and see how you feel. Your dog will suffer more. It can quickly dehydrate and die.

Because I think it is important to understand your Standard Poodle in order to have a reciprocal happy, stable and successful relationship, I have tried, in a later chapter, to give a greater insight to understanding body language.

1 ORIGINS AND HISTORY

Everyone who owns, or is thinking of owning, a Standard Poodle will be curious about its origins. However, there is still uncertainty as to whether the Standard Poodle originated in Russia, France or Germany. It is said that they were, perhaps, more popular in France, for in many places Poodles are known as French Poodles, even today. The Scandinavian Breed Standard notes the Poodle as 'Origin – French'. Certainly the Standard Poodle has always been classed as a cosmopolitan dog living, as it has through the ages, in all parts of the Continent as well as further afield in Greece, Spain, Italy, Britain and, later, in America and Canada. Even in England reference is made to a prototype poodle being used in the Fens around the 15th Century.

It is impossible to gather clear, precise documentation about where our Poodle came from and who was originally responsible for initiating the first selective breeding programme. Perhaps the most authentic and reliable representations of the breed are those that rely on art to paint a picture for us. Of one thing we can be certain. The Poodle and the Poodle Miniature is a truly ancient breed; indeed it is noted that a writer in *Le Chenil* stated that the Poodle appeared in sculpture in the year AD 29, although there does not seem to be any evidence to substantiate this claim. It has also been claimed that Poodles were found on Roman and Greek coins, and they were represented on monuments in the time of Augustus, around AD 14. It is interesting to note that in all early portrayals of the Poodle, he was depicted in a Lion trim, with heavy mane and close-cut quarters – the traditional trim that many Poodles are still wearing in the show ring today.

THE POODLE IN ART

Roland Jones, an author writing in 1848, tells us that the first authentic representation of our breed in art appears on a famous tapestry which is housed in the museum at Cluny in France. The tapestry is one of a series known as The Lady with the Unicorn. Marginally decorated, this historical artwork shows that the hindquarters and half the body are closed-cropped, as in the Lion trim. As for the Poodle in history, this

'Boye' belonged to Prince Rupert of the Rhine and died at the Battle of Marston Moor in 1643. The painting is attributed to Louise, Princess Palatine.

momentous piece of work, if correctly identified, proves that the Poodle, in about 1510, was recognised; that it was a companion of the great ladies of France; that the size was small and that clipping was being practised as long ago as about 500 years.

The late Mr Basil Ionides took a great interest in the history of the breed and was in possession of a magnificent collection of prints of the early Poodle. One of them, dated 1516, is an allegorical engraving after Raphael, presumed to be the Roman goddess Aurora, and at her feet stands a miniature-sized Poodle. An early set of engravings, entitled The Five Senses, of French origin, show a clipped Poodle in the foreground. These engravings are based upon tapestry of the early Stuart period, the reign of James I from 1603 to 1625.

The French artists used the Poodle to depict comedy. There is a print of a Poodle standing, looking hopeful, near the cooking stove of a sausage maker. An interesting colour print engraved after a painting by Henry Bunbury, an English cartoonist, printed in 1803 by Brown of Pall Mall, London, shows an itinerant family of entertainers on the road in Savoy, carrying musical instruments and preceded by a bear straining on a chain to keep up with a Poodle in French, or Lion, trim.

After the Peninsular war, a print was issued entitled Hyde Park which shows Lord Worcester with his Poodle Sancho, whom he adopted at the battle of Salamanca in 1812. This faithful Poodle had been found lying on the grave of his master, a Lieutenant in the defeated French army. This story of devotion proved to be extremely popular and another print was issued showing the dog lying upon his master's grave.

Among the English prints of the period is one showing the Prince Regent in his dressing room, attended by a valet, with a Poodle. More devotion from the Poodle is typified in a coloured print of Louis Phillipe, the last king of France, fleeing with his wife from the fury of the Republicans, and their companion on their flight through the snow is a Poodle.

Although the name Poodle is derived from German origins, there does not appear to be much German artistic history in evidence. However, there is, at the Kennel Club in London, a pamphlet which refers in satirical verses to a Poodle name Boye, who was acquired by Prince Rupert while he was imprisoned in Germany. It tells that this Poodle, the companion of the famous Cavalier, was with him in the battles against Cromwell's forces and that he had perfected the art of catching Parliamentary bullets in his mouth. The pamphlet was published in 1642. Boye was killed at the Battle of Marston Moor in 1643.

Well-known writers said of the Poodle that he is French. Others accredit him to Russia, some to Germany. He was indeed seen in many places on the Continent, but from whence he came remains a mystery. Men such as Thomas Rowlandson and Henry Bunbury were noted for having a sharp eye for a good Poodle and we owe much of our knowledge of early Poodles to such men.

A print of Ceres by the side of a lake, dated 1529, shows a white, clipped Poodle. In 1636 Stern painted The Dancing Boy, a Poodle. A print from 1771 shows a group of professional clippers in France. In 1811 the Prince Regent (later George IV) appeared at court with a Poodle at his feet. Another historical picture shows the Emperor Napoleon returning from the wars and being greeted by his Queen and her Poodle in 1812. In 1823 *The Book of Animals* by Chalons was dedicated to the then Duchess of York, whose love of dogs was well known. On the frontispiece are four dogs, one of which is a Water Dog or Poodle.

POODLE SIZE

We have seen from the print after the style of Raphael, that as early as 1516 the size of the Poodle is depicted as small – miniature. We must therefore acknowledge that the Miniature is not a product of clever, selective breeding by modern-day breeders. The Toy may well have come later, but from the fifteenth century we see both the smaller and the large Poodle depicted. From 1770-1800 Poodles of all sizes are mentioned. Mr Ionides owned many engravings from this period which show the Poodle differing in size as well as being parti-coloured. In the early days there was never an attempt to draw a distinction in conformation between the sizes of the Poodle. And the quality of his characteristics remain the same: he must be strong, active, intelligent and tough, with a smart appearance, and carrying himself proudly, no matter what his size.

Certainly there was a variance in size ranging from the taller, more substantial dog, who was said to have weighed around 40 lbs and was used to pull milk-carts in Antwerp and Brussels, to the smaller, more compact specimens, of more slender and delicate features, which were to be seen on the French boulevards. They were often referred to as the Miniature and the Large Poodle; however, the depicted Miniature variety is often on a par with the small Standard we see in the ring today – but it is difficult to confirm size, where it is not stated, from old paintings and graphs.

The tapestry at Cluny proves that the Miniature size was evident as early as 1510 and well before. This tapestry would have taken years to complete. In Germany and France the Miniature size, thus called, looks to be that of the small Standard. In Russia the Poodle, kept as a house pet because of his amusing qualities, was noted as a very large dog in size.

Writing in German in the mid-nineteenth century, Dr Fitzinger appears to think that the larger Poodle originated in Morocco or Algiers and gives descriptions of six types and sizes which appeared in parts of Europe. In 1861 the writer Meyrick said that, in France, the Poodle was companion to the village sportsmen. He is described as being 15 to 18 inches.

Around 1904 a division of size and coat was implemented at the Kennel Club. Previous to this, all Poodles were classified as Poodles Corded and Curly, ranging from 12 to 24 inches. The new restriction saw Poodles Corded over 15 inches and Poodles Non-Corded over 15 inches.

WORKING AND SPORTING DOGS
Apart from their bravery on the battlefield, Poodles have been noted through the ages for their versatility, in particular their uncanny intelligence when used in water. The name Barbet, which is how the French referred to the breed, comes from 'paddling in mud'. It is said that it was the Poodle's talent for wild-duck shooting which encouraged his introduction into England. Incredibly, dogs which, without doubt, resemble the Poodle were commonly used as Water Dogs in the Fens of Lincolnshire. And, as we have seen, Poodles were used on the Continent to pull milk-carts.

In the book *Hunger's Prevention or the Whole Art of Fowling* by Gervase Markham, 1655, without doubt the Poodle is noted for his sporting activities and great ability for water fowling. The frontispiece shows a picture of a clipped Poodle carrying a bird in its mouth. An engraving dated 1829 shows Poodles being used for fowling in India. In the early nineteenth century, coloured prints of The Cockney Sportsman show Poodles being used for duck shooting

and rabbit shooting.

For centuries, then, the Poodle was known as a Water-dogge. There seems little reason, then, to disbelieve the theory that the Poodle originated from a mixture of waterdogs found in various European countries, most notable among them being Russia, France, Germany and Spain. Many still consider that the early Poodle had marked similarities with the European Water Dog, the Portuguese Water Dog and the Irish Spaniel.

Poodles were also used as Truffle dogs. The truffle is a type of mushroom, sometimes weighing eight pounds or more. Poodles had an uncanny appetite for seeking out the truffles from underground habitats.

THE POODLE COAT
There is little doubt that both the corded and the curly-coated Poodle have been in existence for centuries. At one time, around 1886, it was the corded Poodle which was the most popular. A legendary corded Poodle was the famous Champion Achilles, the first dog to win a Champion status in England. This was in 1890. His sire, Lyris, stood at 21 in height and had spirals of hair measuring 23 inches. Achilles stood at 23 inches at the shoulder and his cords hung 30 inches. The hair on the corded Poodle was never combed, but was continuously rolled and twisted with paraffin and Vaseline to encourage growth.

It is rare indeed, today, to see the Corded Poodle. The coat is tremendously hard work to maintain and most people find it unattractive, but it is interesting to note that the Poodle coat will, even now, if left to its own devices, often form little spirals. Perhaps this verifies the opinion of some breeders from the early days who stated that "there are not two kinds

ABOVE: Janavons My Blue Heaven showing a corded coat. Photo: Diane Pearce.

BELOW: A corded Poodle being shown in France. Photo: Harry Baxter.

of Poodles. Only one. The curly coat of the Poodle is achieved by constant brushing." Mrs Crouch, a popular breeder around 1904, stated that she made up her corded Poodle, Champion the Pilot, then untwisted his cords and combed him out to show him as a curly Poodle. And I have seen this done in reverse – and back again.

The Standard Poodle Janavons My Blue Heaven, from Champion Janavons Midnight Blue and Janavons Rainbows Wish, was shown as a normal curly-coated dog. His owner, Heather Wells, decided to see if his coat would cord. It did readily, as you will see from the photograph of Lennie, as he was known, taken in 1963 by Diana Pearce. Later, Heather brushed out the cords and Lennie was once again a curly Poodle.

As recently as 1997 we saw photographs of corded Poodles in France, taken by Harry Baxter. However, the brush coat of the curly Poodle is the popular show coat of today. I am not sure what the modern judge would feel about judging a corded Poodle. I have a feeling it would be severely discriminated against.

CLIPPING THE POODLE

The clipping of the Poodle, said Gervase Markham in his book of 1655, was necessary because "these Water Dogges naturally are ever laden with haire on the hinder parts; nature, as it were, labouring to defend that part most, which is continually to bee employed in the most extremity, and because the hinder parts are ever deeper in the water than the fore-parts, therefore nature hath given them the greatest armour of haire to defend the wett and coldness; yet this defence in the summer time by the violence of the heate of the sunne, and the greatness of the Dogges labour is very noysome and troublesome, and not onely maketh him soon faint and give over his sport, but also makes him by his overheating, more subject to take the mange."

Markham advised that the heavy coat of the Poodle made him swim less nimbly, and that it was essential for the benefit of the Poodle in his success as a Water-dog to shave the hind parts. Shaving all over was not recommended, as it was considered imperative that the Poodle must have protection on his heart, lungs and chest – "Ayre he shall frize." So, perhaps, here is the origin of the Traditional Lion clip?

It is an interesting fact that the clipping, shaving, or trimming of Poodles has been practised for nearly five centuries. And the Lion clip, as we know it today, historically sometimes called the French clip, has been favoured in the show ring and in fashion for hundreds of years. There are striking pictures of those people who trimmed the Poodles of Paris, both before and after the Revolution. One, entitled Tendreuses des Chiens shows two women, in aprons, sitting beneath large umbrellas, trimming Poodles by the side of the River Seine while other dogs wait their turn.

Canine beauty parlours of the eighteenth century, it appears from artists' impressions, were outside, alfresco. These dog barbers do not appear to have razors among their tools, although it is believed that in France the shaving of Poodles, as distinct from close clipping, was widely practised. Mr Ionides possessed a delightful painting, dated 1701, which shows a party out fowling, and a clipped black Poodle accompanies them.

The Lion clip was depicted everywhere, especially during the reign of Louis Quinze. Early drawings usually show the Poodle with a large mane of hair covering the neck, shoulders and chest, long fringes on the ears and with a profuse top-knot, invariably tied up with a coloured ribbon so that the owners could distinguish their dogs when they were working in reeds. The coat was clipped close on the hindquarters, the rear end, and from the end of the ribs, over the loins and buttock and thigh. Both front and hind legs were clipped close to wrist and hock joint, where hair was left to the toe. The colour of the Poodle was noted as black, white, brown, grey and parti-coloured.

THE POODLE IN FASHION

The early part of the nineteenth century is said to be the golden age of the caricaturists. These artists rejoiced in drawing what they considered to be the foibles of high society. The Poodle was such a prominent figure of social life in England and France that he was a symbol of luxury and became the target of satirical cartoonists. This practice continues today. We have even heard Members of Parliament in the UK referred to as Poodles in a satirical manner in 1996. Those of us who are well acquainted with the Poodle know, of course, that it is a breed that exceeds in intelligence many of the MPs who used the reference in order to intimidate others.

It was said of the post-Revolutionary days in France, and of the Georgian and Regency years in England, that artists engaged in caricature used the Poodle as a symbol to enhance the effect of their drawings. From the works of Rowlandson and Bunbury we owe our knowledge of the fashionable life of the days of George III, the Regency period and George IV. They show that the Poodle was a favourite dog in the boudoirs of England and the salons of France. They were also sought after by the land-owning nobility. The print entitled Bond Street Loungers, dated 1820, shows the Earl of Sefton, the Duke of Devonshire, the Duke of Beaufort and Lord Manners – who is leading his favourite Poodle, Byng, through Bond Street in London.

Because the Poodle is good at playing the fool and rejoicing in a good joke, it easily found its way into the entertainment business. Showmen throughout the centuries have used Poodles to entertain ruling princes and their supporters. It is said that nothing was more natural than the gift of a Poodle as part recompense for the amusement provided by the itinerant show folk. The travelling showman, with the guitar and the dancing bear, had his Poodle. Circuses used troupes of performing Poodles in their programmes. The Poodle was seen as a miniature Dog Toby in Punch and Judy shows. Many Poodles have proved successful in gaining a living for their owners. One was Mirito, who picked out cards and had a good command of arithmetic.

THE 20th CENTURY POODLE
The popularity of the Poodle showed a steady increase from 1918 onwards and was not unduly affected during the 1939-1945 war years, although during that time many breeders had to severely restrict their breeding programme.

In 1934 a kennel was founded in England which proved to be the most historic and significant of all Standard Poodle kennels throughout the world. Mrs Nellie Ionides owned a beloved pony called Vulcan. The kennel was named after him. Nellie Ionides was already the breeder of several breeds of dog when she added Standard Poodles to her kennels. She also added Champagne to their name. Her first sire, and first Champion, was Vulcan Champagne Pommery, which she purchased from the

The Vulcan kennel (left to right): Vulcan Charlotte Purse, Vulcan Black Varnish, Vulcan Mimosa and Vulcan Champagne Volata.   *Photo: Thomas Fall.*

Int. Ch. Nunsoe Duc de la Terrasse of Blakeen: Winner of 18 Best of Breeds, 16 Non-Sporting Groups and 11 Best in Show awards including BIS at Westminster 1935.

Bekham kennels. According to records, the first black Standard born at Vulcan, on February 16th 1938, was Vulcan Black Varnish, by Nunsoe Alaternus out of Skyhigh Sheen. In 1934 Vulcan Champagne Cliquot was born, bred by Mrs Walsh. His colour was apricot, and he was the property of the Hon. Mrs Nellie Ionides, at the Vulcan kennels, which was then registered at Twickenham.

During the Second World War the main kennels to maintain the Standard Poodle with the encouragement of the Kennel Club were the Piperscroft, Nunsoe, Rathnally and the Vulcan Champagne. In the early post-war years some of the kennels at the forefront of Standard Poodle breeding and exhibiting

were: Nunsoe, Jane Lane; Beechover, Miss R. Gregory; Frenches, Mrs R. Price-Jones; Peaslake, Mrs Hilliard; Piperscroft, Mrs Boyd; and, of course, the still resounding Vulcan Champagne, Mrs Ionides, with Shirley Walne who was then manageress. Some other names of consequence were Mrs Fife-Fails, Mrs English, Miss Hocken, Mrs Skeaping, Miss Bowring and Mrs Monroe.

The Vulcan Champagne kennels were a premium kennel during and after the war. Evolving mostly from Vulcan Champagne stock came the famous Frenches kennel and the Peaslake kennel. The Frenches and the Vulcan Champagne dominated the show ring, producing many Champions. Mrs Proctor had a fine kennel of brown Standards, the Tziganes. Champion Tzigane was sired by the brown Champion Vulcan Champagne Darcy, a café-au-lait dog owned by Rita Price-Jones, who was the founder of the world-famous Frenches kennels.

Rita Price-Jones had four bitches of different colours from the Vulcan kennels. Mrs Eckford went to the Frenches kennel for a Standard Poodle to work as well as to show. Mr Eckford's golfing jacket was made into a coat for their bitch, so that her coat would not be

*Vulcan Champagne Cliquot, born 1934.
Photo: Thomas Fall.*

Jane Lane pictured with Chevalier Labory, Int. Ch. Nunsoe Duc de la Terrasse of Blakeen, Mins of Aurelus and Nunsoe Philait Jove.

damaged while she was working in deep thicket. This bitch was made a Champion – Ch. Frenches Maureen. The late Lady Marion Phillips used a Frenches dog to get a good working Poodle. He was used at Crufts by one of the top dog food firms to advertise their products.

One of the most notable Standard Poodles was the International Champion Nunsoe Duc de la Terrasse of Blakeen, who was imported into England from Switzerland by Jane Lane. He was described as being truly elegant and with a great character and is said to be behind most of today's Standard Poodles. He was eventually campaigned to his American title by Mrs Sherman Hoyt after he joined her Blakeen kennels. He was a truly magnificent dog who won 18 Best of Breeds, 16 Non-Sporting Groups and 11 Best in Show. He was also Best in Show at the Poodle Club of America Specialty 1934 and 1936. He won Best in Show at Westminster in 1935, the first and only time that this has happened. Most of the early Poodles in America were imported from the UK. Today America still imports English Poodles – and the English breeders import stock from America.

TALL, DARK AND HANDSOME
The most outstanding import into the UK in recent history was the dog who made a significant impact on British Standard Poodles and, indeed, on Standards throughout the world. He was UK Am. Can. Ch. Bibelot's Tall Dark and Handsome, owned by Susan Frazer. At the tender age of seven months, and in only five days of showing, this amazing dog became a Canadian Champion. At 11 months 'TDH' became an American Champion. Then, with a total of 13 Group Firsts and three Best in Shows under his belt, he departed for England. Six long months in quarantine saw TDH released just three days before the famous Crufts Dog Show. This was in 1965 and he took the Reserve CC. He competed and won at 30 English Shows, totalling 13 Best in Shows. When he retired from showing in 1968 he had 31 Best in Shows in three countries to his credit as well as achieving Highest Scoring on numerous occasions in Obedience.

However, a truly great dog is not just one that achieves success in the show ring. TDH surpassed all expectations in siring not only many beautiful Champions but also many quality

LEFT: *UK Am. Can. Ch. Bibelot's Tall Dark and Handsome: This Standard Poodle took the show scene by storm.*

RIGHT: *Ch. Vicmars Balnoble Royale: An outstanding example of the breed.*
Photo: Diane Pearce.

Standard Poodles that are the foundation of many of the top British lines today.

TDH took the English show scene by storm. Not only was he a great Standard Poodle to look at, with his wealth of beautifully turned out coat, but he had inherited the superbly sweet nature of a great Standard Poodle. A formidable team was made by TDH and his handler, Marilyn Willis. Not only did Marilyn turn out TDH, or Tramp as he was known to his friends, to perfection, she was the epitome of perfect handling. Marilyn possessed a smooth, easy, effortless grace which many of the English handlers still mirror today.

TDH was called small by some Standard Poodle enthusiasts, yet it is interesting to note that, prior to 1930 and the importation of the tall white dog, Triple International Champion Nunsoe Duc de la Terrasse of Blakeen, most British Standard Poodles were 19 to 23 inches in size – the size that is popular on the Continent today. TDH was mated to Pethmely's Bracken Brown and the bitch Vicmar's Legacy of a Legend was bred; she was owned by Anne Beswick.

This bitch was later mated to a son of

TDH, Champion Springet Darken Democrat, and so emerged one of the greatest characters and most superbly constructed dogs to be produced in the UK, Champion Vicmar's Balnoble Royale, bred by Anne and owned by Vicky Marshall. He was a dog that once you met him you never forgot him. He sired many Champions and top quality dogs and his name can be found in most of the top winning pedigrees throughout the world. His progeny is still prevalent in top show winning Standard Poodles today.

The Standard Poodle is bold, wise and tender and unsurpassed as a sportsman, beating all including the clever German Shepherd Dog. He will retrieve, herd, protect and fight to defend. He will learn tricks and play the clown and add gaiety to the life of all who know him. He is fun, loving and quite unique. Wisdom and dignity is inherent in the Standard Poodle, who deserves an owner who will appreciate and cherish and rejoice in his tremendous temperament. He is today as devoted, loyal and delightful as he was at the beginning. Here is to a wonderful companion whose temperament is king!

2 PUPPY CARE

If you do not have a clue where to purchase a sound, healthy Standard Poodle puppy, contact your national Kennel Club and ask for the name and address of the secretary of the Standard Poodle Club in your country. The secretary will then put you in touch with your Area Representative or Puppy co-ordinator, who will help you to find a reputable breeder.

You may meet a Standard Poodle owner who is delighted with their dog and willing to pass you on to its breeder. In the end, the decision whether to buy or not is yours. Visit several breeders, see how their puppies are housed and reared. Meet the sire and dam of the puppies if possible. Most breeders travel several miles to use a good stud dog, so it is not always possible to view both parents at the same time. If the breeder has more than one Standard Poodle it is perfectly in order to ask to see all the dogs, not just the mother of the pups. This will give you a better insight into how the Poodles are kept, and clearer idea of their temperament.

SELECTING A BREEDER

Choosing a puppy from a litter is not always possible. Most breeders have a waiting list of people wanting their Standard Poodles, and often have a certain colour or sex pre-booked. The ideal is to book your puppy early. If the dam is a good-natured, well-balanced Standard Poodle and the sire has been carefully chosen to complement her, all the resulting puppies will reflect this breeding. So-called runts or weaklings, should be rare in Standard Poodle litters. A breeder who has met you a few times, and who knows their litter well, can often choose the puppy which will suit your needs better than you can yourself. I have persuaded a couple with young children to take a certain puppy – they trusted my judgement and a delightful family was made complete.

The secret here, of course, is to have faith in your puppy's breeder. If you mistrust the breeder for any reason, then go elsewhere. Most breeders want their puppies to lead a happy and healthy life and would be horrified to hear that a dog they have bred has ended up on the Rescue, so it is in their interest to match owners and puppies. A caring, reputable breeder will always be there for you, at the end of the telephone. If you are silly enough to buy from a puppy farm or a dealer, you will get no back-up and no certainty of health and quality. What happens to the puppy after it has left the breeder is your responsibly, but a decent breeder will stand by their pups and help out in times of crisis. Sometimes it is just reassuring to be able to talk to somebody that knows.

CHOOSING A PUPPY

Standard Poodle puppies are not shy. They love people and, when you sit on the floor to play, they will climb all over you, chew your shoe laces, nip your ankles, pull at the wool of your cardigan with their piercing, needle teeth, then probably fall heavily asleep in your lap, sighing contentment. Sometimes they will go into a corner to sleep when they are tired or hot; this is quite different to hiding away as soon as you approach.

Think twice before buying a scared or shy puppy. I must admit I have done this. Once because I was naive and so excited about having a new puppy, and again, several years later, with far greater experience under my belt, because I felt sorry for a badly treated puppy. These puppies took a lot of time and attention but the rewards were high and many. I have never regretted it. So again, although most breeders warn you against the shy, diffident puppy, in the end it is your choice. Provided the puppy is sound and healthy, with the right patient treatment it will come round and become a shining example of its breed.

Puppies should feel and smell good. They should not have bulging tummies or feel thin and weak-boned. They must have clear, bright eyes and a healthy substance to the coat. By the time they are six weeks old they should be having free access to the garden or a run; as Standard Poodles are so clean they will virtually house-train themselves by eight weeks if they have been kept clean from the beginning and have access to their mothers for copying and learning. A puppy which does not have access to such freedom, such as a kennel-reared pup, will not have had the opportunity to be so far forward.

LEFT: Standard Poodle puppies are not shy, and so you should be looking for a puppy who is happy to come up and greet you.

RIGHT: Watch the puppies playing together this will tell you a lot about their individual characters.

Regardless of whether you choose a dog or a bitch, the Standard Poodle should be good-natured and eager to please.

MALE OR FEMALE?

The temperament between male and female Standard Poodles should not vary in any considerable degree. Some males are dominant. Some females are dominant. In my household where I once had three males and four females living in harmony together, it was one of my females that ruled the roost. She was not the eldest and did not fight. She ruled through superiority of nature and, at sixteen years old, and now with a household of bitches, she still rules.

The reason I have all one sex now is because of the way we live. All my Standards live in the house with us and when we had males and females, because they were all entire, we had to split them into separate rooms. I do have plenty of space for this but, to be honest, it is quite unfair and the males do suffer frustration. That is the only reason I now have one sex. By way of their heritage Standard Poodles should be companionable and gentle regardless of sex.

When choosing the sex of your new puppy you may have preconceived ideas. If you really want a male, then wait for one, and vice versa. If you can be persuaded either way then you do not have definite views. There is nothing wrong with that. Standard Poodles of both sexes are, and should be, good-natured and friendly and eager to please.

FEEDING

When you take your puppy home you will have, along with the Kennel Club registration, a pedigree, a certificate of worming and a diet sheet. In the UK the Kennel Club also offer a Healthcare Plan for registered dogs. Each puppy is entitled to six weeks free healthcare cover, starting from the moment the puppy is handed to its new owner by its breeder. To qualify for this the new owner must register the transfer of ownership with the Kennel Club within ten days of purchase.

It is probably true to say that most early vet bills are acquired because the over-zealous new owner does not follow strictly the diet the puppy is used to. We all have preferred ways of feeding, which is fine. The problems start when the very young puppy, used only to one food, suddenly gets fed everything under the sun. And yes, it will eat the food keenly to begin with, giving you the impression that it has been starved by its breeder!

There is such a selection of processed dog food to choose from it is no wonder many new puppy owners become confused. Breeders supply a diet sheet and then, when the new owner takes the puppy along for its inoculations perhaps the vet will suggest a completely different diet; then the new puppy owner meets another puppy owner and they are feeding something different again. All say their diet is the best. The poor newcomer to dog ownership is bewildered. Do not despair!

There is no doubt that dogs like a variety of foods. Being natural carnivores they love the internal organs of other animals such as beef (usually complete with well-chewed grass and vegetables), their meat, bones, everything. As natural scavengers they eat anything from scraps to the compost heap. Dogs descend from the wolf and still carry their natural instincts. These instincts are often depressed by an owner who refuses to accept their dog is a dog. I have had Poodles come to stay with me who will not so much as look at a raw meaty bone while there is a human in sight, yet leave the dog alone with the bone and you will soon hear it crunching with great passion. Here is a dog whose owner has made it feel guilty for displaying its natural instincts. In order to please, the dog will suppress these instincts. Standard Poodles love to please their owners at almost any cost.

Today we can buy dry, so-called balanced dog food, tinned food, meat-based foods and cereal-based food, or we can feed dogs as close to nature as we can with a diet of raw, meaty bones, meat, vegetables, fruit, eggs and whatever. Basically, unless a dog has an allergy to certain foods, it will survive quite well whatever you decide to feed.

Dry food is convenient, easy to obtain and store and needs little thought or imagination. But before you decide whether this really is substantial food, mix it with water for ten minutes or so and see how it looks. We are told this food is completely balanced and there is no need to feed a dog more than this. But puppies, and adult dogs are individuals; they do not necessarily all thrive on the same amount of food, vitamins and minerals.

Many dogs have an intolerance to wheat products or, even worse, gluten, which is to be found in wheat, barley, oats and rye. I have a dog who sniffs at all her food and will not be tempted by any means to eat any normal biscuits or bread. If I give her gluten-free bread, or home-made gluten-free biscuits, she relishes them. She is not a fussy bitch. She will eat any meat, vegetables, fish, eggs, cheese etc. I do not know what would happen if I only gave her dry food. No doubt she would eat it when she got starving enough. But why should I argue with her? She has far more superior natural instincts than I do. If her body is telling her no to cereals containing gluten – which, in actual fact, is about as far removed from natural food for a dog as anything – then maybe she has good sense.

Tinned feeds are easy to store, dogs do seem to quite like most of the varieties and they can be fed with a wholemeal biscuit, pasta or rice (rice is naturally gluten-free) as a filler and for variety. Lots of healthy dogs eat tinned meat and biscuits.

The more back-to-nature diet of raw, meaty bones, raw meat, vegetables, fruit, eggs, cheese, milk, and fish may, at first thought, seem less convenient. One needs a freezer to store adequate supplies of meat, one needs a friendly butcher to supply bones, and it is necessary to mash or pulverise vegetables. Dogs, however, thrive on this diet, and they adore it. And once you have made up your mind to feed this natural diet it is only a case of getting organised. It is, in fact, very easy to feed this way. And if some of the latest research figures are to be taken seriously, a dog may be less susceptible to bloat when fed a high meat content diet.

So, where does all this leave the new puppy owner, who is listening to everybody and getting nowhere? May I make a suggestion? Please yourself, at least with consideration to the particular need of your individual dog. If your puppy or dog does not like dry cereal-based food, he will not fare well if that is all you feed. The same goes for any other food. Most dogs have a great deal of good sense before we interfere with them. Before I knew that dark chocolate can cause kidney failure and death to some dogs, I often wondered why it was that most of my dogs always refused chocolate when it was offered. If your dog looks wonderful, with shining bright eyes, blooming coat and it never needs to see the vet, then you are more than likely

doing what suits him. Feed convenience food if you will, but a couple of raw meaty bones a week will only do him good, as well as spicing up his life and preserving his teeth. If you feed your dog sweet biscuits, cakes and cream buns, expect trouble. Obesity, bad breath, digestive problems – and more vet bills.

During my time I have met a great many Champion dogs whose owners tell me they feed their dogs on a bit of everything – and several times a day – some dry food, complete food, wholemeal biscuit, tinned meat, fresh mince, tripe, and scraps.

If your dog is healthy, happy and mentally stable on the diet you have chosen then stick with it. Dry foods are normally very high in protein, which does not agree with all Standard Poodles. If your dog is fed this and it gets hyped-up, uncontrollable and irrational or, even worse, irritable and bad-tempered, then lower the protein in the diet immediately. You will be amazed at the difference.

RECOMMENDED DIET
One dietary factor which must be stressed is that any change of food must be gradual, over weeks rather than days – especially where the dog has only ever been fed one brand or type of food. And two meals are always better than one. Here is a diet I find my dogs are happy with.
Breakfast (after exercise) some raw meat followed by a raw chicken wing or two. Any large raw meaty bones.
Lunch for puppies milk and honey with a little puppy food or scrambled egg.
Dinner Mostly meat with a small amount of wholemeal biscuit (soaked for puppies, or puppy food), greens or any vegetables finely chopped or pulped.
Supper for puppies Diced bread and butter

with milk and a little grated cheese sometimes.

My adult dogs eat about one pound of meat a day total and a small handful of biscuit. A puppy will eat as much, if not more. Puppies must be fed three meals a day, at least. If your dog increases too much in weight, cut down the amount of food, not the feeds. If he is hungry and is not overweight, increase the amount of food over three or four meals. A thin dog will need four feeds a day.

I give garlic (crushed fresh clove or half-teaspoon of powder) which is wonderful for keeping worms and fleas at bay as well as stomach disorders, and brewer's yeast for vitamin B (about six tablets for an adult, and three tablets for a puppy). Two or three times a week they have vegetables, and they like eggs, cheese and pasta and rice as well as some fruits. If you feed this diet you will be feeding a balanced diet over a space of days which is far more naturally acceptable to the dog's construction. You will have a healthy dog with far fewer risks of skin problems, dental problems, eye problems, reproduction problems, or growth problems.

Puppies very rarely overeat when they are fed three or four times a day. They need meat and bones to grow strong. I must stress all bones must be raw. Cooked bones are dangerous as they can easily splinter. Any raw meat is all right for the dog's constitution. Wolves do not cook their meat. Unbleached tripe, chicken, fish, eggs, cheese, and vegetables and fruit are all excellent natural foods. It is easy to feed a dog as nature intended. Bones will provide all the natural calcium required. I have never given calcium additives to my dogs and they have super bone, they look and feel great. Since feeding this diet I have

never had problems with whelping and the bitches produce sound healthy puppies. My dogs live a long time (four of my dogs lived until sixteen years old) and I rarely need a vet for anything other than vaccinations. Vegetables and fruit are an excellent source of vitamin C and should be introduced to a puppy as soon as possible.

If your puppy is happy but does not eat what is on offer he is not hungry. Most people tend to overfeed their puppies. They want them to be constantly eating. Sometimes during the teething period, usually up to six months of age, puppies can develop quite sore gums and refuse their usual biscuit (mind you, they never refuse a bone to crunch on). Have a look at your puppy's gums and, if they look plump and sore, this is why the puppy is being fussy. At this time they can be extremely excitable and nibble everything in sight; your fingers and ankles will suffer if you do not scream out when the pup nips you too hard. A puppy may have a rise in temperature at this time. Generally the pup with teething reaction and a slight temperature will feel quite hot and bothered. This situation should not last long. It is true to say teething problems are unusual, but they can occur.

It is a fact that some Standard Poodles, as with other breeds, do have an intolerance to wheat or gluten, which appears naturally in wheat, barley oats and rye. The dog will often be picky, will refuse normal biscuit, and if it does eat the biscuit, a period of depression and sometimes quite severe stomach ache will follow. There are on the market today – if feeding naturally with meat and vegetables seems too big a burden in a busy working day – gluten-free feeds. I have used these very successfully on a bitch I have, which I have never bred from, which suffered spasmodic colic when fed even the slightest amount of wholemeal biscuit.

Always have fresh drinking water available to the dog.

ARRIVING HOME

When your puppy is eight weeks old or more, you will be able to take it home. Amid the great excitement it is easy to forget the pup's first needs. It is surprising how many people think that the first thing they should do is feed the new arrival. Do not, not yet. The very first thing you must do is introduce the puppy to the place where it can relieve itself. Little puppies have tiny insides and they cannot hold on for any length of time. After a car journey your puppy will be keen to spend a penny. If you take your new puppy straight into the house and put it on the floor it will puddle on the carpet. Go straight into the garden with your puppy and wait with it until it has emptied its bladder, then let it follow you indoors.

The puppy will play and explore and you will be obviously paying it at lot of attention, but, after a few minutes, go back outside with pup following. The pup will then know its way around and the correct place for its toilet. Even puppies as young as eight weeks old do not make many toilet mistakes, providing they have been correctly reared by the breeder, and given a considerate owner. Never smack or shout at a puppy if it makes a mistake; a grumble will do the job without further chastisement. Harsh treatment at this stage will set your puppy back weeks, maybe even months.

As I have stated, it will not be necessary to give your new puppy a meal on its immediate arrival; better to wait and let it explore, maybe have a little sleep. When you do supply the meal, do not be over-generous. A puppy may get an upset tummy just from leaving its secure environment, without it being overloaded with strange food. I say strange food, because it is surprising how many new puppy owners ignore the breeder's diet sheet and feed all sorts of things the puppy is not used to within hours of having it in its new home.

If you change your pup's diet as soon as you get it home, do not be surprised if it has diarrhoea the next day. You are then straight up to the vet's, into a waiting room full of sick dogs, and you wonder why the puppy is suddenly ill. Another grave mistake new puppy owners make, having been brainwashed by the media, is that they rush out and buy worming preparation. Look carefully at the worming dates given to you by the breeder, and at the date the puppy is next due to be wormed. Follow the directions. Worming preparation is poisonous and overdosing can cause serious damage to the insides of a tiny pup.

SLEEPING QUARTERS

You will already have decided where the puppy is to sleep – but good intentions were made to be broken. Most people cannot bear the cries of a puppy left on its own for the first time in its whole little life. To go to bed and leave the poor thing for eight hours is cruel. I have never been able to understand why Poodles have to sleep away from their owners. My husband Roy and I have always allowed the puppies that we keep the freedom of the house, and we have rarely had a puddle, not even from a six-week-old who decided she wanted to sleep with us rather than with the rest of the litter. All our Poodles have duvets, which are easy to wash. If you are determined that the puppy must sleep downstairs, it will help if you have another dog to keep it company. If not, a fluffy toy is helpful – with the eyes taken out to prevent the puppy swallowing them. If the puppy cries for ages it is doing so because it is severely distressed, so expect an upset tummy in the morning.

Be sure to get out of bed first thing in the morning the moment you hear the puppy wake, whine or start to yawn and take the puppy outside immediately to relieve itself. Also do this immediately after each meal and during play, and every time it wakes from a snooze. Puppies that do not sleep in your room are much more likely to make a puddle during the first few nights. The best thing is to get up the moment you hear it moving about, then pop it out to spend a penny and you will both feel happy. If the puppy is not in your room you could leave newspaper down on the floor. It will more than likely be tired on its first night and sleep like a log, unless it is worried. Standard Poodle puppies need to sleep a lot to maintain the energy to grow. In your room the puppy will sleep well all night.

TRAINING

Standard Poodles only need love and food and company, then they settle down very quickly. It is a good idea to socialise them with other dogs, children and people as soon as possible. Take your puppy out in the car, to meet friends, as well as having friends come round. Leave the radio or television on so the puppy hears lots of noises and friendly familiar voices. I leave the television or radio on for the pups all day from day one. When

Int. Swed. Fin. Ch. Janavons Ballerina aged twelve weeks.

they leave for their new home I let the new owners know which programmes they are used to hearing. That way they are at least used to one familiar thing in the new home. My pups wake up with Radio Two's Sarah Kennedy! I leave the radio or television on for the adult dogs when I go out. It's a habit.

At eight weeks old your puppy needs to start its training in socialisation. It cannot, of course, go for walks; as well as being too young, it has not yet been immunised against infectious diseases. Do not be frightened to take your puppy with you to friends etc., but be certain any dogs you come in contact with are healthy and have been vaccinated. Young puppies are best left to exercise themselves in the garden by playing with you. At eight weeks you can gently

Plan a training programme for your Standard Poodle from an early age. This puppy, Papuska Starlight Express To Acecliffe, went on to become a highly successful competitor in Agility.
Photo: Bob Ratcliffe.

to sit, and to stand, and to lie down, to walk beside you on the lead, and to come (for a tidbit or praise) and it must learn to sit still on a table and be brushed.

While your puppy is teething, sometimes up to six months of age, it may not always be sensible when you want it to be. Be patient. Dogs, like children, can have a difficult time with their teeth. If your Standard Poodle pup does get very excitable you should look at his diet. Are you feeding too much protein?

When teaching a Standard Poodle you will find it will learn very quickly if you make sure you get it right. For instance, if you want your puppy to come, it is no use whatsoever shouting at it. Call the puppy with an excited tone and give it lavish praise when it comes. Laugh and clap your hands. Run the other way so that your puppy runs after you. Do this at a very early age and your puppy will soon get into the habit of coming to you. Never chase your puppy. Even from eight-weeks-old your puppy must come to you. Playing hide and seek in the house and garden is a wonderful way to get your puppy to come to you, especially if you clap your hands and laugh when he finds you. Obedience is habit. Get it right and the habit will be installed for life.

Lead training is easy when you have another dog for the puppy to follow. If you do not have another dog, first introduce the collar. When the puppy is used to this, slip the lead on and let the puppy walk around with it in tow. Do this a few times, then take up the end of the lead loosely and use your loving voice to encourage the pup to follow you. If the pup bucks, drop the lead and run a few paces forward. Your pup is used to following you so he will do this

throw a ball a short distance and a Standard Poodle pup will retrieve it.

Keep walks short for the first five months and then restricted to reasonable length until the puppy has reached full maturity. This will ensure sufficient care of joints and bones, and will not put any strain on them which will cause problems in later life. Certainly do not be tempted to take up any form of serious training like Obedience or Agility until after this age, or your Poodle will suffer for it later on. You may teach your pup now and you must praise him well. Then take up the lead and try again. Standard Poodles are very clever and they learn quickly. Your puppy will soon grasp what it is you are asking. If you feel exasperated, forget training that day. You will only go backwards with puppy training if you get cross. Do not forget, Poodles are clever, they can read your mind quite well; think right and your Standard Poodle will act right.

GROOMING AND TRIMMING

Grooming is an essential part of a Poodle's life. The Poodle is blessed with a woolly coat that does not moult. This is the reason asthmatics are not allergic to Poodles. The coat must be brushed daily and trimmed regularly. Your puppy will have had its feet, face and tail clipped and been bathed by the breeder before it comes to you. If you live a reasonable distance from your breeder then you may well be able to return the puppy for its trimming each four to six weeks. If not, you must visit local Poodle trimmers and find a kind, sympathetic, experienced groomer for the clipping, unless you mean to learn how to do this yourself. And why not? Get your dog's breeder to teach you if you can.

Brushing is far easier to cope with than trimming. This must be done daily, or at least three to four times a week. It only takes a minute or two to brush a Standard in puppy trim; your puppy surely deserves that much of your time. Always try to use a table for grooming, it is so much easier. Have a table placed against the wall to begin with, so that you have more security with the young pup and more control. A rubber mat is a good idea to prevent slipping. Car mats are inexpensive and do the job admirably. Pop the puppy on to the table.

One word of warning here. If you use a domestic table, such as the dining or kitchen table, do not be surprised to find, when the puppy has grown and can jump, that the dog will get onto the table of his own accord and lie on it. Better to use a table which your pup will know is his, perhaps in a utility area.

Take a pin brush or a slicker brush and carefully but firmly brush through the coat; then take a wide-toothed comb and comb through the hair. This must be done all over, paying special attention to behind the ears and under the arms, where these parts seem to tangle more as the puppy gets older. When the job is done, make nice noises at your puppy, telling it how handsome or pretty it looks. A young pup will soon come to enjoy being groomed. Take care to stand close to a young puppy when it is on a table for they are sometimes quite wriggly and you must not allow it to fall from the table. Never tie a puppy or dog to a hook on the wall, or anywhere else. Dogs have been strangled this way.

BATHING

If you wish to bath your puppy then use a mild shampoo; baby shampoo or frequent-wash shampoo is fine. Be careful to keep ear flaps down when spraying water, and take care not to get shampoo in the eyes. Be vigilant about rinsing. Many novices leave traces of shampoo in the coat and then wonder why the puppy is itching after a bath. Use mild shampoo and a conditioner. The puppy or adult Poodle will need careful drying. This is not a breed one can wash and leave to dry. The coat hair must be thoroughly combed through when wet and brushed or blow-dried until completely dry. If you leave the hair wet, a puppy could get dangerously cold and the hair will mat if not groomed properly. Do not hold a hand-drier close to the puppy's eyes. Use it on low speed and ensure that it is just warm on the head.

With a pet trim it is relatively easy to keep control of the coat, provided the dog is trimmed regularly. New Poodle owners are often shocked that a Poodle needs to be trimmed so often, but I can assure you this is so. The coat hair grows very quickly and needs constant attention, rather like our own hair. Do be sure to brush and comb your Poodle properly before and after washing it to prevent mats and tangles from forming.

Good shampoos are essential to keep the coat healthy. Some are very harsh and strip the coat of all the natural oils; the dog begins to itch, the owner thinks the dog has fleas or something, and so washes the dog again in harsh shampoo, or some dreadful violent insecticide shampoo, and hey presto! creates a skin problem. If in any doubt at all, use baby shampoo. If you would not put the shampoo on your head, certainly do not put it on your dog!

EQUIPMENT
Most pet shops and garden centres sell pin brushes, slicker brushes and wide-toothed combs, which is all most pet owners require for everyday grooming of a Standard Poodle. If you intend to clip your Poodle yourself, you can purchase all the necessary equipment from one source. Ask your breeder for the address of a supplier or buy one of the dog papers or magazines where you will find advertisements from suppliers. No matter where you live in the world it is relatively easy to buy a dog paper from a newsagent, or through the post.

It is not a good idea to learn trimming on a puppy. You will get frustrated and the poor, naturally excitable puppy will suffer for it. Better to find a good, experienced trimmer who is willing to help you. (Do not expect this advice for free.) There are courses available, but they are very expensive and there is the risk that you may not take to trimming at all and you will have wasted as much money as it costs for your dog to be trimmed for a couple of years. Far better to choose your breeder wisely and have a few lessons with them. While some Poodle owners quickly pick up the rudiments of trimming, others find it an impossible task and take their dog to the Poodle Parlour for its whole life. There is nothing wrong with this, provided you are in a position to pay. Poodles must be trimmed regularly, about every four to six weeks. Most show dogs are trimmed and bathed every week.

INOCULATIONS
All puppies need some form of immunisation to protect them from infectious diseases. I must stress that all puppies do need some form of protection from diseases, and to vaccinate and run the risk of a few dogs reacting is far more beneficial than not to vaccinate at all. I have to say I am becoming more and more sceptical about today's method of injecting multiple diseases into young puppies with only one or two shots. It seems we have more and more vaccines and more and more diseases. Is there a connection? We now dose puppies as young as eight weeks with a variety of diseases – Leptospirosis, Hepatitis, Kennel Cough, Distemper, Parvovirus. Does this cause too much strain on the immune system of some puppies, causing it to break down at some stage? I do not know the answer,

In no time, your Standard poodle will be an integral member of the family.

but I do know we have problems in dogs we have never had before, relating to the immune system. Many puppies have seemed perfectly well and then, after a dose of multiple vaccines have been introduced, they get a temperature and become ill. Teeth suffer and we see more and more dogs with the brown vaccination stain associated with Distemper.

I do not mean to scare people away from vaccination, but just to consider the point of spacing out vaccinations with less strain on the immune system. In a later chapter I have looked more closely at vaccination reaction and the use of nosodes as an alternative. Please do make sure your puppy gets some form of immunisation. The question I ask is: Should they be given so many lethal doses in two or three injections? I now insist on a longer course, with the Parvovirus given alone. And I never vaccinate before twelve weeks because of the way my pups are reared. For extra safety, to ensure we are not overdosing the immune system with unnecessary diseases, there is a test called the 'T Test' which you can ask your vet to do. Perhaps we should all consider this.

3 *UNDERSTANDING YOUR POODLE*

When I was a child most of my friends and neighbours owned dogs. Not a dog, because invariably they had more than one dog. Those dogs, like the dogs in most of the countries of the Continent today who are lucky enough still to have a society that chooses to ignore European rules and remains welcoming to dogs entering shops and restaurants, came and went throughout the house and garden. They curled up in the kitchen beside the cooking range or beneath the table where food was being prepared, and they drank from our cups as well as eating scraps from our plates. At night the dogs slept on our beds, or somewhere near. As we did not have central heating in most houses, the dog in winter was a godsend – far superior to any hot-water bottle, or the dangerous electric blanket that replaced it.

The dogs survived healthily on scraps, meat and vegetables, were rarely bathed or wormed, and they joined us kids in the park or on the common for romp and play. We were never troubled by health fanatics frantic to order us to do their bidding, and condemn our best friend; and neither we nor our dogs needed shrinks! Or, as we call them today, Animal Behaviourists. And – would you believe it? We live to tell the tale!

Like man, the dog is a social animal. And, in particular, the Standard Poodle is

It is essential to establish your role as pack leader.

Photo: Carol Ann Johnson.

gregarious. Neither we nor our beloved breed are fitted for practising a solitary life. As with its predecessor, the wolf, who lived in groups and packs, in companies or organised communities, the dog is interdependent and co-operative to company, respecting those of superior rank or experience.

THE PACK ROLES
In the wild the wolf still lives in groups and packs. Each pack has a head, leader or boss, or a pair of leaders – a male and a female – who keep order through combining skill with facts and events. Experience. Greater knowledge and intelligence. They do not keep order through aggression, as some folk may think.

Dogs must have a rank leader in order to live in harmony and concord. If they challenge and fight it is because their boss, or leader, has not afforded them a sufficiently subordinate role. There is a tremendous difference in loving one's brother and letting one's brother run amok. If you make a special fuss of a young dog, while at the same time failing it by not teaching it standards or rules, it may well challenge the principal. What happens is that you, as the boss, afford too much privilege to the youngster and it is then under the impression you wish it to take over. Elders, or leaders, should accept the privilege of their position. We are our dogs' leaders. Through voice control of tone alone we maintain discipline. In conjunction with body posture, that tone denotes leadership and superiority. Dogs, raised properly, will not challenge that. There is no need for physical force or aggression when training a youngster. You must know that you are the boss, the leader, the chief, and you will be.

The Standard Poodle is a big active dog, and so you will need to establish a code of acceptable conduct. Photo: Steph Holbrook.

TEACHING THROUGH PLAYING
When you play ball with your puppy you throw the ball, the puppy fetches it. You praise the puppy when it returns to you with the ball in its mouth. You ignore the puppy and walk the other way when it carries the ball off with the intention of making you run after it. Do this in a safe area such as your securely fenced garden so that you can concentrate on play training without worrying about the untrained pup escaping through gaps into danger. If you start training in an area where you are panic-stricken that the pup will get out if it does not come immediately, you will be teaching it a good lesson in how to have you running round in circles. Life is just a game to a young pup. You must have higher intelligence and use this game time to teach lessons in obedience.

On a walk your dog must come when called. You should not be chasing after your dog, or shouting unduly – dogs have acute hearing. This bond of trust and obedience starts with your gentle puppy training. You run slowly away from an eight-week-old puppy and it will quickly follow. You praise it for doing so with nice words in an encouraging tone – Gooood Boy! Gooood girl!

If the puppy ignores you when you are calling, you go up to it, and push it, as its mother did in the nest. Then, as soon as you have its attention, you call in a pleasing tone. When the puppy responds you laugh, and praise it. Not many Standard Poodles can resist coming to you when you laugh. The reason why some handlers can get the best out of every dog they train or show is because they are happy with themselves and confident in what they are doing. Dogs feel secure with a person that is self-possessed.

You feed the dog, as its mother did; you groom the dog, as its mother washed, licked and groomed it. You take over from the mother as the head leader. A tidbit can be used for reward, but mostly your praise and pleasing tone of voice is all a dog requires to establish your relationship. You call the shots, the dog responds and receives praise for doing so. Happy dog and happy owner. This is especially true of the Standard Poodle.

Because humans are easily intimidated they allow themselves to be controlled by dogs. Some people get nasty and blame their dog for all its behaviour inadequacies, others get frightened out of all proportion. I once had a call from a distressed husband whose wife was lying in bed with a Toy Poodle on her chest. This little dog growled each time its owner tried to move. She was frightened to get up. I went to the house and just gave one calculating look at this little

dog. It immediately jumped off the woman's chest. This confused little dog was strangely glad to see me. I felt a bit sorry for it: it was totally at a loss, completely confused by over-indulgent owners.

All owners must be kind; do not ever feel guilty about petting and loving your dog. Love it to bits, but do not confuse it by being paranoid. And do allow it some space. All dogs, like the rest of us animals, like to let off steam and expel excess energy. Do not expect total devotion to extend to a dog never leaving your side or having fun. All dogs should have the freedom of a good gallop, or time to play and enjoy exploring in the garden, making friends and playing with friends.

Every now and then you can call your puppy in from its chosen entertainment with an excited voice. It will come immediately to see why you are acting so interestingly. Praise it, give it a tidbit and then allow the puppy back to its pastime. Often, I call a puppy (and my older dogs) when they are in the garden, and when they look to see what I want, I run away, upstairs or into another room, hiding behind the door. They love it when they discover my whereabouts and we laugh. This is a terrific game that teaches 'come' so easily. I also do this when we are out walking, pretending to walk one way and allowing the dogs to run so far, then I dodge behind a tree or run away like mad the other way. The Poodles come hurtling after me and keep an eye on me for ever after.

DOMINANCE AND SUBMISSION
This wonderful game reinforces the lesson the puppy learned when you trained it to come by walking away and praising it when it came to you. It is of

Standard Poodles will enjoy being kept together, but you must ensure that they are prepared to submit to your authority.

no use whatsoever waiting until you puppy is ten months old, then letting it off the lead, waiting for it to get out of earshot and then calling it until you are blue in the face. If you have taken on an older dog that has got into bad habits through lack of sensible training, then you must go right back to the beginning. Go back to basics and train in a confined space on the lead, then on a longer lead, being sure of control before letting it off the lead. In the garden, of course, the dog can be free, but use the caller method of excitement, tidbits and praise to teach it to come when not on the lead.

With the untrained dog on the lead (a long lead) call the dog in with a tweak on the lead to gain its attention and praise it. Allow the dog to go out again and recall. Keep doing this at odd

intervals and the dog will soon get the message. Repetition will instil discipline. Standard Poodles learn their lessons very quickly.

EARLY SOCIALISATION

Standard Poodles are happier when they know where they stand. They are extremely easy to train and are easily domesticated. If your pup has been reared properly by the breeder before the age of eight weeks, your task as its new owner will be made considerably easier. The pup should be accustomed to other dogs – its litter mates and parents, uncles and aunts. My puppies mix with all my other dogs as soon as the dam is willing to share them (more on this subject in the chapter on breeding). Standard Poodle aunts and grannies love puppies. My puppies are house-reared, so they are used to the radio and television, visitors and children. The lack of early socialisation is the greatest cause of behaviour problems. Many people leave a puppy until it is six months old before they start training in socialisation. This is far too late. The pup should be mixing from the time you get it – as it should have been before you purchased it.

When I hear of Standard Poodles being frightened or untrustworthy with children I despair. What on earth has happened to the dog for it to react in this way? Apprehension of children can be credited to lack of early socialisation with kind children. Children and Standard Poodles should be a natural progression to growing. Do not, however, leave any dog alone with children you are not fully acquainted with. Some children can be extremely teasing and accidents can happen.

The same applies to Standard Poodles and cats. Introduce your dog to cats as soon as possible. Dogs and cats should be friendly; when they are raised together they like each other's company. The trouble only starts when a dog never has a chance to get socialised with cats, and is even permitted, or encouraged to chase them. The only time that I do not completely trust my Standards with unknown cats is when they have new-born puppies. Some mothers are very protective in the first week after whelping and may attempt to attack anything other than their nearest and dearest in order to protect their young.

Remember, when you take your puppy home, it has never known loneliness. Your puppy has so far lived its entire life with litter-mates, friends and people that love it – assuming it comes from a reputable breeder. The most natural thing in the world is for the puppy to cry, or yell, or bark or howl the moment it is left alone. This crying is the natural, instinctive, distress call applied with intelligence and good sense. The bark, call, or whining is to inform the family, or the litter-mate, or the dam or friends, of anguish: 'Help! I am lost, come and get me!'

It is totally unnatural, even cruel, to leave a puppy alone for any length of time; it will soon become shy, fearful, over-excitable and, in extreme cases, aggressive. This behaviour is the result of isolation. If you only have one dog or puppy and you must leave it alone, then you must build up the time gradually and always leave the dog with the company of the radio or television, as well as supplying safe toys and raw meaty bones for entertainment.

UNDERSTANDING ANXIETY

It is perfectly natural for a dog to be claustrophobic; they hate to be left alone in a confined space. When a dog is mentally tortured through the effects of isolation it will resort to chewing the furniture, messing, or howling. Certainly it is considered that more dogs die of loneliness when in quarantine than through any illness. Many people are under the illusion that a dog is naughty because it is bored, when all that is happening is that the dog is reacting to anxiety and fear. Just for the record, a dog is not capable of revenge. They do not chew your slippers, or rip the carpet to get back at you. Remember, dogs descend from wolves not humans!

If you leave your dog for some time alone, and it does something to displease you, it will sense this displeasure the moment you walk through the door. It will know if you are thinking, 'What has he done?' The dog will hang its head, lay back its ears, lick its lips, and tuck its tail under its body. The dog may crawl along the floor on its belly. Some people are under the impression the dog knows he has done wrong and is feeling guilty. This is not the case.

The dog that cringes and crawls on its belly as soon as its owner walks through the door is attempting to soothe its owner from the anger it senses, by using submissive behaviour. The dog cannot understand why its owner is angry or displeased; it just knows from instinct that you are. If you understand how distressing and unnatural it is for any dog to be left in isolation, you may have more patience when it does something you consider wrong every time you go out and leave it. Remember the radio, the bones, the toys, and allow your dog plenty of space. Nothing is comparable to human company, but these things will help. If you shut a dog up in a small room, it is quite likely to go mad in a short space of time. No dog should be left alone all day, every day. And certainly not a Standard Poodle.

MUTUAL UNDERSTANDING

Standard Poodles do like to use their mouths for expressing their feelings. They like to hold wrists gently between their teeth and lead people about, displaying their fine goods for all to see. The Standard Poodle also likes to jump up and lick your face, showing its pleasure about you. It is not a greeting enjoyed by everybody. If your dog jumps up, try to turn away from it and then pet it when it has all four feet on the floor, or is sitting down. Dogs jump when they are happy or to gain attention. Standard Poodles are deliriously happy when their owners return from an outing. However, do not confuse this greeting with the dog who goes berserk when you walk through the door. Ask yourself whether you are rejecting your dog in some way if it is so overwhelmingly desperate for your attention.

Puppies use their mouths a lot to explore objects, whether the object is you, a child, another puppy or a piece of furniture. If your puppy bites you too hard, you must cry out loudly with shock, it will soon realise it has been too rough and will be more gentle next time. Teething puppies are sometimes in a very 'I want to bite everything' mood. Offer the puppy an alternative to your hands or clothes; a soft rag of its own, a toy or a bone. Deflect its attention by rolling a ball about on the floor. The puppy will soon grow out of this phase of biting – but do make sure the ball is so big that the puppy or dog has no chance of swallowing it.

Because the most important thing in a Standard Poodle's life is to please its

The Standard Poodle is biddable and will enjoy training sessions.

owner, it will very soon discover the things that achieve this. Poodles love laughter best of all. When teaching a Standard Poodle something new, if you clap your hands and laugh and smile at its pleasing behaviour, it will be in raptures and become very obedient. Shouting and smacking never achieved much more than making a Poodle confused and nervous. Ignoring a Standard Poodle for a short time is chastisement enough. And do remember that you are talking to a foreigner when you talk to your dog. Choose your words carefully and speak clearly with tone, backing the words up with signals.

TEACHING SIT

Sit is quick; it is a command. To teach Sit, push down on the base of the tail to achieve the position (never in the ribs, or just below, where the kidneys are located). Another method of teaching Sit, is to use a piece of liver or cheese. Hold it in your right hand just above the pup's head. When the pup reaches up for the tidbit its head will go up and its bottom down. If you say Sit as this is happening, repeating it three or four times a day, your puppy will know Sit after a few days.

TEACHING STAY

I always teach a puppy the Stay on a table. Being careful to be near enough to prevent the pup from falling over the edge, I put the puppy, as young as eight weeks, on the grooming table (which is against a wall on two sides) brush the pup for a moment or two, then tell it to Stay for a second or two while I stand close. If the pup comes towards the edge I push it back and repeat Stay. A clear, calm command. It is amazing how soon a pup learns this message. Do not, however, leave a young puppy unattended on a table. And never, as I have said before, tie any dog to a hook in the wall – it can so easily hang itself. With a little patience from a sensible owner a Standard Poodle can easily be taught to Stay, Sit or Stand on a table without jumping off.

YOUR RESPONSIBILITIES

It takes time to learn a foreign language and, although Standard Poodles are highly intelligent, they are not born with a dictionary in their heads. If your Standard Poodle is not responding properly, it is you who is at fault. You must be clear, decisive and patient.

Time spent playing with your Standard Poodle is valuable. Play is an important part of all our lives. If you have two Poodles they will play together endlessly. Sometimes, when a new puppy is

LEFT: . Sit is a quick, easy command and is useful on many occasions.   Photo: Carol Ann Johnson.

BELOW: It takes a little practice to learn the Stay command.   Photo: Steph Holbrook.

imported into the household where there is only one other Poodle, the older one may take a few days – sometimes longer if it is closely bonded with its owner – to accept the puppy. But within a few weeks these two will be the best of friends and the older dog will be happier for the friendship. Do not worry if the older dog puts the pup in its place sometimes. This is a natural form of teaching authority and will establish pecking order. Playing with you will strengthen the bond between you; play hide and seek – which teaches Come – fetch, jump hurdles (for the older dog), and tug-of-war. If your young Standard Poodle needs confidence, let it win at tug of war often. Likewise, a dog displaying over-confident behaviour, on the verge of challenging, only needs its owner to straddle it, putting a hand under its chest to lift the front end off the ground, for it to submit.

Standard Poodles learn quickly. They learn from us. We teach them to pull on the lead by pulling them. We teach them not to come when they are told by not bonding with them sufficiently and then scolding them when they do eventually come. We teach them to be frightened of things – children, thunder and fireworks – by our own reaction to these things. If your Poodle shivers at a noise and you comfort it by saying, 'It's all right, there's a good boy,' you will be praising it for being scared. Better to laugh and sing and ignore the noise. Your dog will soon forget about being scared once it realises you are not worried.

BODY POSTURE
Body posture is important in the relationship between human and dog, and dog and dog. Standard Poodles are demonstrative in displaying body language to express their thoughts. I once had a Standard staying with me whose owner said it was terrified of the postman and tried to bite him. I have not got a clue what started this unwelcome behaviour, but the dog never did it when staying with me. On its first day, at about the time my postman calls, I opened my front door and allowed the dog out with my eldest, and top-ranker in the hierarchy, Pollyanna.

All staying Poodle visitors are put to the floor by Pollyanna the minute they walk through the door. She stands, head across their shoulders, touching sometimes, and rumbles deep in her throat; some well-chosen words are being stressed, I am sure! If not enough of a response is forthcoming, if the dog is choosing to ignore the reasonable warning not to overstep the mark, then she grabs their neck with such speed and effectiveness that they roll over to the side, away from her. The ultimate in submission is when they continue to roll and complete the resigned attitude by lying on their back with all four feet in the air. Pollyanna insists they know who is boss around here, even at fifteen years of age, and if anybody dares to argue with her, which I must say is rare indeed, then, before she offers to kill them, I step in and inform the lesser dog that when I do not give the orders around here, Pollyanna does. I do this with a crumpled, prune-like face and a tone of voice resembling one who has the considered opinion that the dog must be plain stupid to challenge such authority.

Now, back to the postman. I let the dog out with Pollyanna and, as he raced to get to the postman, she was onto the dog and got him floored before I could ever have done so. Once she considered the lesser dog had been properly dominated, Pollyanna left him to squirm while she made a big fuss of her friend, the postman. Thankfully our postman is a dog person and he later allowed the dog to make friends with him. All the time he did this, Pollyanna was watching carefully out of the corner of her eye, with an obvious spark of severity. Her head was held high and her body was fairly taut.

Because the Standard Poodle is so intelligent and learns very quickly from us, we have to think seriously about what we are doing to make them react in a way that we find unpleasant. A short time ago I got a call from a distraught owner whose dog had the habit of emptying the waste bin whenever she went out. Because the dog knew, by the exasperated tone of voice and the sharpness of her actions, that she was in some way unhappy with him every time when she came home, the dog took to wetting on the floor as soon as she came through the door.

To remedy this I suggested three things; that she give the dog a raw meaty bone to chew in her absence, that she remove or empty the bin before going out and that she allowed the dog more freedom through the house and not to be enclosed in the kitchen.

It was imperative to change the attitude of her body language before the dog retreated further into an incurable nervous breakdown. Once this was explained, the owner saw the error of her ways. This dog was acting out its ancestral characteristics, those of a natural scavenger, and rummaging through the waste bin. Her disturbing behaviour in reaction to this perfectly normal function unnerved him. His reaction was not only peeing on the floor, but curving his body away from

her when she shouted at him, and constantly trying to lick her. Dogs lick to promote attention. They also nip to get attention. They learn this when playing with their brothers and sisters.

COME AND PLAY
Standard Poodles use great body posture in expressing thoughts. There are many different attitudes stated in play. The Standard Poodle's facial expression fairly smiles when it wants a game. Its eyes widen and look full of fire. It licks its potential playmate – usually us – on the face if it can get there. Its head bows and the shoulder swings sideways, quickly allowing the rest of the body to follow so that the rear end is quickly shown, to dispel any implication of threatening behaviour. A Standard Poodle characteristic is to dip its front end, sometimes with the chin on the ground, with its bottom raised in the air, its tail wagging high and wide. They do this to another dog or to you. It merely means, come and play. Sometimes added to this charming display is a squeaky bark.

One characteristic that always makes me laugh is, for instance, happening now. I have been typing for some time. I start early in the morning, for that is the time I am at my best. My Standards loll about on my bed or on the settee in my office, which happens, for my convenience, to be next to my bedroom. For a time all is well, then there are a few yawns and stretches from the Poodles. Then one of them, usually Penny or Goldie, pushes open the curtain with its nose and makes a sudden, exciting bark, as if to say "Look here quick!" The others join in, but I know their game and I have not finished yet. I tell them to be quiet for another ten minutes, to which the reply comes 'who-oo-oo-oo'.

In other words: "I am fed up with you typing, it is about time you stopped and took us for a walk." When I promise to do so in one minute all goes quiet again. I do not break promises, for they would soon get to know!

Another display for suggesting play is to bounce towards you, or another dog, with a smiling face, tail wagging, then raising one leg and pawing and patting, then nudging the hip against the playmate. The tail wagging from side to side, the bottom often going with the motion, means one happy Poodle.

TAIL WAGGING
Short, sharp wags of the tail can indicate challenge to another dog. Sometimes the hair and skin along the spine will be raised all the way down to the base of the tail. This display of primeval arousal can signify the dog is ready for a challenge of authority to a newcomer, or that it is feeling sexually confronted and is feeling confused about it. Once the situation has been clearly assessed by the dog, the hackles will return to normal.

The tail wagging is, of course, widely recognised as showing a display of pleasure. But that is not always the correct translation. It depends on the height and the degree of the wag as to what it really means. As we have established, a good, side-to-side, high wag means the dog is happy. Short, rather stiff movement could imply caution or restraint. The low hanging tail, close to the body, shows a display of severe uncertainty, a lacking in confidence. The tail might be very high, banana-shaped or even attempting to curl over the back, which could mean the male wishes to challenge another male.

FIGHTING
Dogs and bitches will occasionally argue, even with their same sex. Properly raised Standard Poodles normally only need voice remonstration from their owner in order to back off. Males that are raised together from puppies get on incredibly well. The best way to deal with a real fight that is out of control is to walk away from it. Alternatively, you could try throwing a bucket of water over the fighting pair; the shock very often parts them. You beating and shouting in a panic will only aggravate the situation. Owners should apply dominance from puppyhood onwards to prevent challenging behaviour.

CHALLENGING BEHAVIOUR
This is best dwelt with early on. Stand over the dog and lift its off-side foot off the ground, push at the shoulder nearest to you to roll the dog down, and keep it down for 30 seconds or so. Reward submission verbally; rebuke struggling with a stern voice.

Then stand straddled over the dog and lift both its front feet off the ground by placing your hands under its chest. Keep it off the ground at the front for 30 seconds.

Go through set exercises of sit, down, stay, heel for about five minutes every day or at least twice a week with the dog on the lead. Always reward with voice and tidbits for good behaviour. Rebuke with a deep, gruff tone and signs of dominance.

JUMPING UP
Poodles love to dance, and play and jump! It is quite a good idea to dissuade jumping up when the Standard Poodle is young. To do this, simply turn away from the dog, ignoring it, displaying

your dislike of such action by turning away from it. When the dog comes with four feet on the ground, praise it. Unfortunately we often, without thinking, teach the dog to jump up by clapping our hands in the air, or raising a tidbit high as soon as the dog comes for it. Jumping should be discouraged, except when it is done by request. A Standard Poodle who has been in some way excluded from love by a member of the family, or who has a complex because it is not understood and treated as though it is wanted, will often develop the habit of jumping up to try to lick the face for attention. It jumps up because your face is so far up. To get attention from its mother, or from the pack, it would merely have to lick their face. A Standard Poodle such as this needs to have its owner look into what can be done to improve the dog's role in life to make it feel more secure and wanted. Licking faces is a way of showing

submissive behaviour. Taking a Standard Poodle to good, kind, training classes in Obedience, Agility, or even just Good Citizen Test, is a way of forging a bond between dog and owner.

Another charming habit of the Standard Poodle is to nose-poke. It pokes everything – from the washing-machine, to the doors leading from room to room, to food it is wary about, to play items, to you and all your friends. They poke with their long noses also to give you a kiss.

Teach with play. Be understanding. Watch your Standard Poodle and learn. I hope I have given you a little knowledge about the language of dogs so that your relationship can be more satisfying. Love your Standard Poodle and it will repay you with total loyalty. Have fun with this fun-loving dog, and deeply enjoy the pleasure of the fabulous Standard Poodle.

4 COLOURS AND TRIMS

Standard Poodles come in many colours. Black, blue – or gray as it is called in some parts of the world; the English spelling is grey – silver, silver beige, chocolate brown, brown, café-au-lait, apricot and cream and white. Colour genetics is a fascinating but often confusing subject. Talk to many breeders about mating big B to little bb and they immediately look bored and perplexed. This is not the book for a complicated analysis of the genetic constitution of the Poodle; however, out of pure interest, we will look at some of the colours and I will try to explain in simple terms why it is that some colours can be safely mixed together, while it most undesirable to mix others. We will also look at some Champions in many of the different colours.

QUALITY OF COLOUR

The coat must be an even colour at the skin. This is slightly confusing, as coats do show varying shading in young dogs and some colours, such as blue, or gray, being carried on a black line, will sometimes take up to a couple of years to arrive at their final colour. If a bitch of three years, of a fairly substantial blue colour, is mated, the bitch's colour after the birth of the pups will lighten considerably, sometimes to such a degree that the bitch is considered silver. Some of the colours may show varying shades in parts. In blues the ear fringes are often lighter, quite silver in fact. In browns and creams and apricots the shading may be darker on the ears. With cream and white the ear fringes are frequently dark apricot/cream in young dogs. White and cream dogs are often born a deep apricot colour. This colour, however, will show a much lighter shade at the skin, certainly by the time the pups are a few weeks old. This change of colour in young puppies is often the reason novice breeders, and those not so well acquainted with colour breeding, register their puppies as the wrong colour.

Clear colours are certainly preferred, but natural shading is not considered a major fault, especially while the colour is clearing. Parti-coloured, or dogs not of a solid colour (black with white toes and chest; black with brown markings) are disqualified in the show ring. This does not make them a less fabulous pet.

Standard Poodles with such markings are fairly rare; they must not be used for breeding. Dogs used for breeding should be from solid colours only. Shading is quite different. Red shading in a young black or blue changing coat is often seen and not disqualified, as this is a perfectly natural process. The sun will highlight red shading in black or blue.

DEFINITION OF COLOUR

A black is a solid jet, hard black. Sometimes the untrained will call a blue Standard Poodle black. But there is a major difference. A true blue or gray as an eight-week-old puppy has a silver-tinted face, obvious when the face is closely shaven, whereas the black has a jet black face. Put the two together and you will quickly see the difference. A blue, whose body coat as a puppy is black, should be showing signs of clearing from a young age and should stand out as a blue/gray by twelve months. Without question, a good blue will be just that, from an early age, on its face. The coat, when uncut, may be still quite black, but the clipped parts are distinctly blue.

Usually natural colour progression changes from the bottom of the legs upwards. This can especially be seen in a young silver, whose body may be still quite dark blue and the legs silver. Do not confuse this natural blend of colour with the dog that is of two colours, which is most incorrect. Blue is a dilution of the black gene. Mate blue to a good black and you will lose the blue colour in most of the puppies in the first generation. Then put one of these puppies back to black and you will lose the true colour of blue altogether.

If you are a novice breeder it is important to know the pedigree of the dogs you are mating and to give serious consideration to colour. To retain colour, mate black to black, or blue to blue, or blue to silver. Black and blue with white ancestors can be mated to white. It is probably impossible to find a pedigree with entirely one colour breeding. There is nothing wrong with that, providing the right colours have been mixed.

Silvers have a distinctive silver face (like stainless steel) usually by six weeks of age. Again the body colour can take varying times to clear. This is perfectly

LEFT: *Silver – Aust. Ch. Neiger Circus Rose CDX.*

ABOVE: *Blue (left) and Silver – clearly seen as two separate colours.*

permissible. It is advisable to mate silver to silver, or silver to carefully-bred blue. Mate silver to black and you will lose the wonderful silver colour.

A silver beige, born from silver or blue parents, is very pretty indeed but fairly rare and often confused with café au lait. The silver beige colour, which resembles a rather rich tea biscuit, is descended from brown being introduced to the line at some point. The puppies are born quite reddish-brown. They have a distinctive beige face at eight weeks. Care must be taken when breeding this colour to keep well away from any white/cream breeding. Silver beige has brown pigment which it will pass on to white and cream. This is totally unacceptable.

Chocolate brown is rather like plain dark chocolate, but this can vary and lighten or turn rather red in the sun (a red not to be confused with the dark apricot colour now called red). The lighter brown is perhaps more commonly seen and more of a ginger colour. Mate brown to brown, or brown to black where the ancestors are known to be brown, or brown and black. Never mate brown to white or cream. If you do this, the pigmentation will suffer in the form of brown or pink eye-rims, lips and nose in the white/cream – totally incorrect. It is not advisable to mate brown to a black which has white in the

Silver/Beige – This colour is rare, and can be mistaken for Café au Lait.

ABOVE: *Brown – Representatives from the Tragapanz kennel in Sweden showing a chocolate brown shade.*

RIGHT: *Ch. Albareas Rufus is light brown in colour which can look almost ginger.*

pedigree. The liver pigment of the brown will come out in the white and cream resulting from such disastrous colour breeding. If you care about this lovely breed, do not mix brown with white or cream.

Café au lait is brown that is complemented by such close cream hair that the coat still shows as a solid colour. Hence coffee and cream! A clear café au lait is most attractive but rarely seen in the show ring. Mate to same colour or darker brown or brown-bred black. Never mate to cream or white. Pigmentation in eyes, eye-rims, lips and nose will suffer, resulting in a loss for the breed.

Apricot is distinctively the colour of an apricot. However, a lighter shade does exist. It is far safer to mate apricot to self-colour unless expert advice is sought to use a blue or black. This will

invariably lose the colour in the first generation but is useful when a fault needs to be eradicated and when more substance is required. I do suggest that anybody debating cross-colour breeding of apricot seeks advice on pedigrees from an experienced apricot breeder. Apricot lines today are stronger in quality. Apricots have been born rusty black, otherwise they are deep red.

The red colour being seen in the show ring in many countries today, and which

Janavons Madelaine Belle shows a red shading in a brown coat.

ABOVE: Apricot – A most distinctive colour, though it can appear in a lighter shade.

LEFT: Café au Lait – Janavons Vulcan Heaven Knows. The brown colour is complemented by cream hairs to create a solid colour.

is becoming increasingly popular, is a deep, dark apricot. Cream is rather like a white, enhanced with a pinkish/beige tint. Shading of dark apricot, or darker cream, is usually seen on puppies, especially on ear fringes and very often in a streak of almost apricot colouring along the spine (back). This darker shading clears to an even colour with maturity. Mate to self-colour or to white, or to black from black/white breeding. Mating cream to brown lines will result in a decline of the pigmentation, resulting in a decline in the quality and premium characteristic of the breed.

White is so pure – when clean – that it almost hurts the eye to look at it, especially in sunlight. Mate white to white, white to cream where the pigment is substantial, white to black from black/white breeding or white to blue. Do not ever mate white to brown.

White: This is a sparkling, pure colour. Photo: Carol Ann Johnson.

All colours have their magnetism. Some people do have a preference for a certain colour. Black with white hairs, known as salt and pepper, is not a true solid colour. However, blacks often fade with age and they invariably have white hairs here and there. An odd grey or white hair is ignored in a show dog, but bad colouring – when the colour is not solid in the main – is considered a fault.

PIGMENTATION

The pigmentation of the Standard Poodle does vary with the colour. Brown, and café au lait, and silver beige have liver-coloured noses, eye-rims and lips, with dark toe-nails and dark amber eyes. The black Poodle and the blue, silver, cream and white, have black noses, eye-rims and lips, black or self-coloured toe-nails and very dark brown eyes. Apricots should have dark eyes and black points; however, in some parts of the world, liver points and amber eyes are acceptable.

Sometimes a cream or white will suffer from a slight fading pigment of the nose in winter and after a bitch has had a season. This must not be confused with inferior pigmentation. Brown or pink nose and eye rims in cream and white is not permissible.

SKIN COLOUR.

All browns have brown skin. Black and blue have dark grey or blue skin. White and cream should have dark silvery skin; however, where the mane protects the skin from the daylight, this skin may remain pink in some whites, even where the points – nose, eye-rims and lips – are black. Dark skin is tougher and more desirable and far less trouble than the lighter pink skin, which can be sensitive.

TEMPERAMENT

With the variation of colours it is true to say that temperament does also vary somewhat. Browns are generally more clownish and slower to grow up. Blacks are a little more staid. Whites are often quite sensitive. Blues are clever and soft. However, it is impossible to generalise. Standard poodles are often bred from two different colours, black/white for instance, or black/brown or blue/white. And all the colours are beautiful.

COAT CARE

BRUSHES

There are so many brushes and combs on the market that it is easy for a newcomer to get mind-blown when looking through a catalogue or the stands at a show or in the local pet shop. The curry brush or, as it is often called, the slicker brush, is most often used for pet coats. This is a wire claw-type brush set into a rubber base. It is quite a good brush for getting through thick coats; do not, however, use this on the body where it is clipped short. Here you must use a slightly softer brush such as a pin or bristle brush. For the long show coat, a pin brush with whalebone or nylon pins set in a rubber base is best. Grooming is essential, but you do not want to break the hair off when you are desperately trying to grow length for the show ring.

COMBS

The best comb for all coats is the wide-tooth steel comb. There are combs which have wide-spaced pins at one end and closer-placed pins at the opposite end. These are the type I use. Some groomers prefer a comb with a wooden or nylon handle.

PUPPY GROOMING

When you purchase your puppy you will need to start a daily grooming routine. Your puppy will have had its feet and face clipped by its breeder and will have had its first bath before you call to collect it. Now it is up to you, and the more frequently you attend to grooming, the better for you and your pup. A couple of minutes a day is all that is required to accustom your new puppy to being brushed and combed. Like us, Poodles do enjoy looking good, so they readily accept grooming. If you take a little time to groom daily then your task will be fairly easy. Only when the coat is changing from puppy to adult will you find the grooming is a little more arduous – when the fluffy hair comes out, to be replaced by a stronger, more coarse and dense, more springy coat which, when it is complete, is actually easier to groom.

The young pup's hair is easy to brush and comb and, because of this, some owners think there is little need for a regular session of grooming. But I urge you to get into a routine. Once the coat gets to the matting stage – anything from seven months onwards – then suddenly to try to start grooming is tough work on you and your Standard Poodle. From the age of eight weeks your puppy can have its face, feet and tail clipped every two weeks.

ADULT GROOMING

When brushing or combing or bathing and clipping, stay with a system. Start on the head, grooming away from the eyes, down the ears, being careful to include the hair behind the ears where it is more likely to tangle. Brush down the neck and along the body towards the tail. Brush the tail. Next, starting with the right foreleg, brush up towards the ribs from the toes, then section from the bottom and comb through each layer. Do the right hind leg; turn the dog, saying 'Turn' as you do this, so the dog will soon learn what is expected and turn on command.

Continue grooming the front left leg, then the left hind leg. Brush lightly but thoroughly, taking care to include under the armpits and inside the legs – places often missed by novice groomers. Part each section of the longer hair and be sure to brush to the skin. Very often a dog looks beautifully groomed until one gets one's hands into the coat, only to realise then that the top ends of the coat are groomed but that the dog has a felt-like mat at its skin. Pet dogs should not suffer the discomfort of matted or felted hair any more than the pampered show dog. These felts, or mats, are disastrous to a show coat. Poodles must be shown in good coat condition; there is no excuse for a matted coat.

CLIPPING NAILS

I prefer the guillotine – scissor or straight – type nail-clippers to the ones that cut like nippers. The nipper type seem to squash the nail rather than slice quickly through it. Many dogs hate to have their nails cut because they are tender. Take care to cut only the very end so as not to damage the quick and make the nail bleed. On a white nail it is easy to see the quick inside the nail. It is a vein which is dark because it is filled with blood. A great deal of distress will be caused to the dog if you cut into this quick. On a dark or black nail more care must be taken. Usually, if you put slight pressure on the nail clipper too near to the quick the dog will pull its foot violently away from you. Try again, this time taking less nail. Dogs

Nail Clipping: Cut a small piece of nail at an angle going with the growth of the nail.
Photo: Steph Holbrook.

that have good feet and regular exercise on roads or rough ground rarely need to have their toe-nails cut, but if you must see to this, try to have an experienced groomer with you when you first attempt this operation. Certainly have some permanganate crystals handy in case you cause any bleeding. These can be dabbed on to the end of the nail with a piece of cotton wool and held for a moment until bleeding stops.

Take the foot in the left hand, placing a finger beneath the nail. With nail clippers in the right hand, cut a small piece of nail at an angle going with the growth of the nail. Repeat with the other side of the nail, taking two cuts rather than one. This way you are less likely to cut the quick and cause considerable pain. Ideally, you could use a firm file to get rid of excess nail. For this you hold the dog's paw in the left hand, the file in the right hand and file the nail from the bottom upwards. Filing is far more natural and I find more effective. It just takes a little more time.

EAR CARE

Tweezers used on dogs' ears are rather like the tweezers we use to pluck hair from our eyebrows, only they are longer for easier handling. However, they are best used only by those who have had expert guidance. Some people do pluck the excess hair from the ears with their fingers. If you attempt this, be sure to take tiny segments at a time, or you will cause severe pain to the dog. As a precaution against ear trouble – canker – it is as well to dust the ears with ear powder every six weeks or so. I have found, through experience, that the less I poke around in ears, the less trouble there is. I check my dogs' ears during grooming and at bathtime but I rarely pluck the hair. I do this only when it is essential. I had a Standard Poodle for fifteen years who never had her ears plucked and she never had a problem with them, ever. Where infection or mites have invaded, deal with it immediately you see brown caking or smell an odour. I use Thornit on all the dogs that come to me with ear trouble. Persistence and proper care will clear the trouble within five days or so. A regular dusting will then keep trouble at bay.

TEETH-SCALING

My dogs all chew bones, and this is an essential part of keeping teeth clean. If dogs are not allowed regular raw bones then dog toothpaste may be required to clean the teeth. Where there is an accumulation of tartar, this will have to be dislodged with a tooth scaler. It is not

If tartar accumulates on the teeth they will need to be cleaned with a tooth scaler.

a nice job but it is better to tackle this yourself, if possible, rather than have a full anaesthetic at the vet's. Provided tartar is not entrenched, it will chip off quite easily with a tooth scaler or even the ends of a pair of closed scissors.

Hold the muzzle with your left hand, putting your first finger into the dog's mouth, behind the canines. Using the scaler with your right hand, chip off the tartar. Gums can be swabbed with a mild solution of peroxide or mouth-wash. Please do not confuse the brown ring stains of vaccination reaction with tartar. If you are unsure, ask an expert. Or give the dog a raw meaty bone and it will take care of the problem itself. Teeth that have been neglected for years will need veterinary attention. Show dogs, or Standards with opulent ears eating raw meaty bones will need to have their ear fringes propped back with a pony-tail band; or better still, cut a head scarf from the legs of an old pair of tights and pull this over the dog's head.

BATHING
Some people may only own one or two dogs which they do not object to putting into their own bath tub. Whether you

have a proper trimming room with its own bath for your dog, or you use your personal tub, a rubber bath mat will be an essential piece of equipment. In order to get a good finish on your clipping and scissoring as well as grooming, your Poodle needs to be scrumptiously clean. Most Poodles enjoy their bath and you must insist they stand still while this toilet is carried out. I use a bath that is waist-high. I have my grooming table beside the bath for ease in getting the Standard Poodle in and out of the bath. Some people have a ramp which their dogs walk up to get into the bath. If you have a good back and strong arms you can, of course, place your arms around the chest and back legs of the dog and lift it into the bath tub. Back pain, however, seems to get us all in the end. Always use a spray or shower unit to bath your Standard Poodle. It is impossible to get the coat adequately wet and rinsed just using jugs of water. Good shampoos are essential. Some shampoos are very harsh, stripping the valuable oil out of the skin and subsequently causing the dog to itch and scratch. If you are unsure, use baby shampoo.

Before starting the ablutions, be sure

your dog has its ear flaps down, or to be on the safe side, pop a little cotton wool just inside the ear to prevent the water and shampoo from entering the ear canal. It is also a good idea to groom out tangles before bathing, if necessary using an anti-tangle spray. With some coats it is easier to split felts or tangles with the finger-tips when the hair is wet. Hopefully though, because you have taken care of your Standard Poodle's coat, it will not have mats or felts in its hair at bath time.

Wet the hair thoroughly; with the full coat it is advisable to wet from the base of the body upwards, otherwise the water tends to run over the top of the coat without making it sufficiently wet. Next, using a squeeze bottle, distribute the frequent-wash shampoo systematically over head, down body, legs and tail, adding water where necessary to encourage a good lather. Be sure to work the shampoo in thoroughly, in order to wash right through to the skin. Some points that novice bathers miss is under the tummy, under the tail and inside the ear leather. And do take care not to get shampoo into the eyes.

Once the coat is well lathered and feeling clean, start the rinsing. Do be sure the water is warm. Rinse systematically from the head, tipping it back to allow the water and shampoo to run away from the eyes. Rinse the ears, down the neck, the body, legs and tail. Do be sure to rinse underneath, lifting the full coat to ensure that each layer of hair is thoroughly free of all traces of shampoo. Rinse, rinse, and rinse until the dog is squeaky clean. Shampoo left in the coat will encourage scurf, it can make the dog itch, and sometimes even cause eczema. Rinsing a large coat takes time. Double check that all shampoo is

removed from the coat before allowing the dog to leave the bath tub.

For a dog that is extremely dirty, a second shampoo may be required. Apply conditioner if necessary. If a dog has a dry coat or skin, use an oily-based conditioner, or add one teaspoon of coat oil to the conditioner. Massage well in, then rinse. Your Standard Poodle can be bathed as frequently as required with no fear of damaging of the coat. In fact, clean hair grows faster than dirty hair and is less likely to break.

DRYING THE COAT

If you keep a Standard Poodle as a pet you will probably have its hair cut short into Sporting or Lamb Trim. In that case you may be satisfied with one of the many hand-held dryers on the market, although I still advocate that life in the grooming room is so much easier with a stand dryer for all coats and trims – they are worth every penny you spend on them. The average price of a good stand dryer is roughly the price of a pup. You may think this is rather expensive to start out with, and, while your pup is very young, you can get away with using your own hair dryer, being careful not to hold it too close to the puppy. Your puppy will feel the heat more intensely than you. For the keener groomer, and for those wishing to show as well as those who wish to make life easy, a good stand dryer is essential because it leaves you with two free hands to work on the dog.

The pet dog can be dried using much the same procedure as for grooming. Having completed the thorough bathing, and having towelled the dog well, allow the dog to return to the grooming table. More towels may be necessary to soak up excess moisture from the coat. Turn on the dryer and groom the coat from the foot upwards, brushing continuously until each section is thoroughly dry before going on to the next. Blow-dry until the hair is dry and fluffy. Then comb through the hair with the wide-tooth steel comb to ensure all tangles are removed. With a hand-held dryer it will be necessary frequently to put down the dryer in order to use two hands to brush the coat through. Matting will result if the coat is not thoroughly brushed and combed during drying.

The show dog will need to lie on its side during the drying of the mane and body hair. Brush from the skin outwards, taking tiny segments of coat at a time, to blow and fluff dry. One word of warning. If you do not dry the coat thoroughly it will curl and prove more difficult to scissor to a professional finish. For those show coats that are difficult and curl no matter what, there is now a straightening spray on the market. This, however, is fairly expensive to use. Better to get the knack of correct drying procedure. It may be necessary or beneficial to spray water into the coat if it is drying too quickly; this will help prevent the coat from curling. Another way to keep hair moist until you are ready to work on it is to leave a damp towel over it.

GROOMING A SHOW DOG
Grooming a show dog takes a lot more time and effort than grooming the pet trim. Start, when the puppy is fairly young – from eight weeks onward – to lie the show Standard Poodle on its side. Later, it will be essential, when brushing and drying, to have your show dog lie quietly in this way. Get your potential winner accustomed to this at an early age. Lie the puppy on its side with gentle firmness, rub its tummy to get it to relax.

Then brush for a moment or two, praise with nice noises in your voice, then allow the puppy to stand up. When the show dog or puppy is accustomed to the table, start the brushing procedure.

With the dog lying on its side, part each section of the show coat from the base of the chest up. Make a definite line from one end of the mane to the other, then brush the section, then comb through gently with your wide-tooth comb, splitting any felts with your finger tips, or using an anti-tangle or oil-base spray to encourage felts to separate. Complete one side, then turn the dog over and repeat the process.

Brush out poms and take care to remove top-knot bands and groom this hair daily. Also, in the older dog with long ear fringes which are wrapped for protection, it is essential to unwrap the fringes and brush through thoroughly. Having completed the essential grooming, gently fluff hair up towards the head to give an appearance of a fluff ball. All show dogs must be prepared and presented in tip-top condition. This is impossible unless care and attention is paid to regular grooming.

TO OIL OR NOT TO OIL
When people ask me whether they should oil their Standard Poodle, especially through coat change, I have to be rather non-committal. It really does depend on the coat. I have oiled coats with unsatisfactory results – especially whites – and I have oiled coats with good results. Rather like the brushing – you can sometimes not do enough, or you can do too much.

Standard Poodles that have their coats oiled need to be bathed on a regular basis every seven to ten days. Oil does prevent matting, where the coat was matt-free to start with, and grooming is less essential. But the oiled coat collects more dirt, and there is the danger of breakage and itching, and it is extremely messy on the furniture. The coat, in general, is far easier to handle and grows better when it is clean. Dirty hair is more brittle. Matted hair breaks when the hair is dematted. If you want to grow a show coat, then every care must be taken to keep the hair clean, healthy and free of matts or tangles.

Taking out the tangles that have formed overnight on a dog which is suffering coat change needs care. Often, it is more beneficial to bath the dog and then split the wet hair with the fingers. Wet hair is more pliable and not quite so susceptible to breakage. Comb with a wide-tooth comb, never a fine one.

Use a good conditioner and, if the coat is very dry, you could try oiling. Mix two teaspoons of the correct type of oil with a cup of conditioner and half a gallon of warm water. Pour it through the coat. I do this from the bottom of the ribcage up, parting the hair as I go to ensure that all the layers are conditioned and the solution has not just run over the top. Some groomers advocate leaving this in the coat, not rinsing it out. When preparing a coat for the show ring, use the conditioner without the oil and rinse.

WRAPPERS
As the hair grows, the ear fringes will need protecting and maybe the topknot and neck hair. The hair must be kept out of the dog's eyes at all times, or you will have a dog with constantly running eyes. As soon as your puppy has enough hair, tie it up with a rubber-band. When the hair gets that little bit longer you can use pony-tail ties or wrappers. Ear fringes can be wrapped, though you must be

As the hair grows, the top-knot and ear fringes will need protection.

Photo: Steph Holbrook.

careful and ensure that the leather is free from any bands. You can use polythene or cotton wrappers but do make absolutely sure that your Poodle gets used to these when you are around. Until the dog has got accustomed to having these strange things on its ears, take them off when you are not going to be present. Some dogs grasp wrappers in their mouths and chew them off with disastrous results. They take the hair with it.

To wrap the hair I start with putting a band in the fringe, being very careful to check that none of the ear leather has been incorporated, as this would cause severe discomfort to the dog and has even been known to sever the lower part of the ear. When the dog is used to the band, use either a polybag or specially-bought wrappers to wrap up the ear fringe. Then roll the wrapper up two or three times and secure with a rubber band. Check by putting a comb through the hair below the leather to ascertain that the leather is free. Wrap the top-knot in much the same manner. As the hair grows you may find two, or even three, wrappers are needed on the top-knot.

LEARNING TO TRIM

Poodles' coats need constant attention. If you have to pay a beautician to clip a Standard Poodle every four to six weeks it can prove to be a very expensive outlay. You can ring round for prices, but do be sure to choose a trimmer who likes the breed. Find a kind, competent trimmer. Standard Poodles should enjoy their visits to the hairdresser.

You may decide to learn how to clip your pet Standard Poodle yourself. If you intend to show, I would say it is essential to learn to trim the dog yourself. The best thing to do is to get your dog's breeder, or an experienced trimmer, to show you the way, then take lots of practice. Standard Poodle people are mostly very friendly and helpful, you will find somebody in your area who will assist you. Or contact your Standard Poodle Club area representative; you will find the address through the main Club or your Kennel Club. I do not advise anybody to learn to trim on a puppy. All puppies wriggle and you could become exceedingly frustrated, which will do neither you nor your puppy any good at all. Even the most perfectly behaved dog can react nervously to a novice trimmer, pulling its feet away continuously when normally it sits as still as a statue. If you do not own an older Standard that is used to being coiffured, then do try to

borrow one when setting forth on your first venture into trimming.

There are books which give step-by-step trimming advice, but I have never yet met anyone who learned to trim with just the aid of a book. The problem is that dogs are not statues; they move about all the time. Learning handling skills is every bit as important as learning to do the actual clipping. Before you go rushing out to buy expensive grooming equipment, such as electric clippers and a power drier, do try to borrow some for your first few lessons. It is better to find out if you are suited to the job before spending vast sums of money.

Setting up is expensive, but the rewards of trimming your own dogs are many. Trimming is a most satisfying and worthwhile experieince.

CLIPPERS

Clipping comes easily to some, while others have to work extremely hard to get good enough results to walk out into the street with the dog, let alone win with their charges in the show ring. The whole procedure becomes less terrifying and less of an ordeal with practice. If you really do not enjoy clipping your Standard Poodle it will probably be better for you and the dog if you take it to the Poodle Parlour. For those with burning ambition I will try to help you, although I still advocate that watching a live performance is also essential.

All trims require the feet, face and tail to be clipped so we will deal with these first, before looking at other trims and how to do them. Firstly, having established that we have a good, solid, stable table, standing in a sensible position, preferably against the wall in a corner so that the learner trimmer is more effectively in control, we will need a good pair of clippers. I know you can go to the superstore and buy a job lot of clippers and scissors etc. for peanuts, but this is a complete waste of money. Very often these clippers vibrate with such vengeance that the poor dog thinks it's having an epileptic fit when you apply the things to its face. They will also make your hands numb after a while and, as novice trimmers are very slow, this will be most off-putting.

Buy yourself a decent pair of clippers. I use Oster and Esculape which are nearly the price of a pup, including the blades required, but they last for ever. For training a novice I like to use Oster as I find them lighter and more gentle and I prefer the way the 15 clips the face, leaving it smooth without grazing the skin. I must stress now, blades must be kept clean and well-sharpened by a qualified sharpener. If your blade ever comes back from the sharpener in less than satisfactory condition, return it immediately and complain. I have known blades come back so sharp they cut skin. I will not tolerate this. However, this is unusual, so we will assume all is well.

Good clippers can be purchased easily from manufacturers or dealers who advertise in the dog papers. They are also for sale at virtually every dog show. With Oster, the A5 is the clipper I recommend. You will need a number 15 blade for the feet, face and tail. Where a dog has a thick coat, a number 30 may be required to get a clean finish on the feet. These blades are detachable and easy to clean using the solution that comes with them. If your supplier does not offer this cleaner, ask about it, and the running oil required to keep the blade as cool as possible. For a pet trim the addition of a coarse body blade is

required, usually a number 5 or 7. I use a 5 in summer and a 7 in winter.

SCISSORS

Next you will need a pair of good-quality hairdressing scissors. If you attend a Championship Dog Show you will find stands which sell scissors along with all the grooming equipment you will ever require. At these stands one is able to try out several pairs of scissors and find a pair to suit one's pocket as well as being comfortable to handle. I find it impossible to order scissors from a mail catalogue because their action does vary so. What is comfortable to one may not be for another. At today's prices you will need to spend about forty pounds or twenty-five dollars for a pair of scissors. You will see them on sale from about twenty pounds to over one hundred!

A GUIDE TO CLIPPING

Okay, you have your gear, so let us get going.

Apart from the feet, always clip hair going with the grain of growth. On the face you will notice this is away from the eye. It is always best to clip clean hair. This is far less likely to cause skin irritation from the clippers. If you clip too closely, apply a soothing lotion or cream – baby lotion, talc, or benzyl benzoate.

One word of caution, when you are learning to trim you will naturally be very slow, so take care to check the blade for heat by placing it on the back of your hand, or on your arm; if it feels more than a little warm do not continue clipping until the blade has cooled. You could burn your dog and make it nervous of trimming for a long time to come. Lie the clipper on the cold floor for a while and do something else while

GUIDE TO CLIPPING
Photos: Steph Holbrook.

LEFT: A white Standard Poodle before clipping.

1. Clip the hair around the top of the foot.

2. Turn the foot backwards (towards the tail) and clip underneath.

3. Fold the ear back over the head and clip towards the corner of the ear.

4. Clip from the eye towards the muzzle.

5. From the base of the ear, clip down to the point of the throat.

6. Clip downwards from the base of the tail towards the tip, leaving enough hair to create a pom-pom.

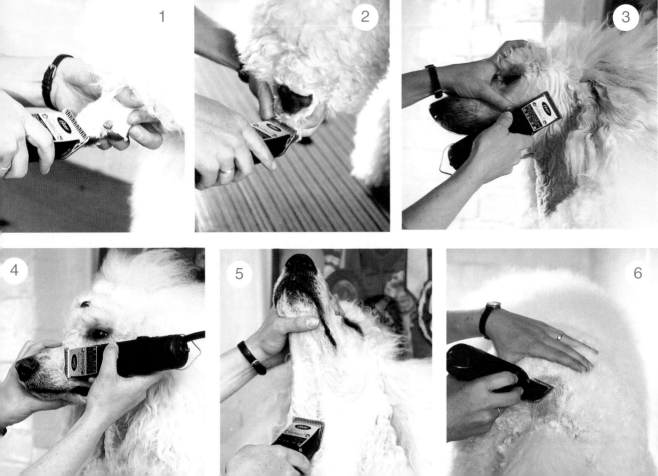

you are waiting for the blade/clipper to cool.

THE FEET

Nearly all dogs have ticklish feet, so they tend to wriggle or pull the foot away from you when you start clipping their toes. However, most get quite used to this in time and cooperate well. It is best to hold the foot reasonably firmly, but do not squeeze it. We clip the hair the opposite way to which it grows. Starting with the rear right foot (being sure that your poodle is standing square and is comfortable) hold the leg just beneath the hock joint, just above the foot, taking care to keep the dog's legs beneath the body; if you pull the leg outwards towards you the dog will be uncomfortable and will fidget.

Gently press the toes apart with your second or third finger and clip all the hair between the toes as well as possible, taking care not to ram the clipper into the webs between toes. And do take special care not to twist the dog's foot as you clip. It is essential to learn the knack of turning your wrist every-which-way in order to complete a neat job of clipping the feet. It is your wrist and hand that must manoeuvre the clippers about; the dog's foot should never be twisted to accommodate you. Clip from the toe nail up to the base of the toe. At first you will probably find this most difficult, but with practice it will become second nature, with a bit of luck. I do not know why it is, but some people never feel easy with clipping. However, most enthusiasts find it satisfying and calming to trim out a Standard.

Now turn the foot backwards towards the dog's tail and clip underneath the foot. Toes, or feet, are clipped to about a thumb's width from the large pad of the

foot. Better to leave the clipped area low rather than take too much off and make your dog look as though it has chicken feet. Now to the front foot. Sit or stand the dog – some dogs prefer to lie down – so that it is facing you; take the lower leg, just below the back pad, in your hand and clip the toes as with the back foot. Turn the dog to make it comfortable and clip underneath the foot.

THE FACE

With clipping the idea is to gently shave the hair to keep it short. The hair should never be shaved so close as to damage the skin. The clipper blade must remain flat on the dog. Do not dig into the skin, or use the tip pushed into the skin, or you will cut it, with possibly disastrous results. I have seen Poodles with their faces cut to pieces, and covered in scars. This is extreme cruelty.

Take the muzzle in your left hand, fold the ear back over the head. From the outer corner of the eye, place the clipper on the face and clip towards the corner of the ear. Next, clip from under the eye to the inner corner, then from between the eyes to the tip of the nose. Now clip from under the eye towards the muzzle, to the nose. From the base of the ear, clip down to the point of the throat – the adam's apple. Clip upward under the lower jaw towards the nose, taking care to tighten the skin of the lips to get a clean shave and prevent splitting the skin. Some whites, with a sensitive skin on their face, may need a coarser face-blade such as a number 10. Thankfully the unhealthy moustache is now considered dreadfully old-fashioned and is very rarely seen. Do be careful to tighten any loose skin with your fingers before running over it with the clippers.

Tighten the skin of the throat by lifting the head upwards to stretch the neck.

THE TAIL

In comparison this is the easy bit. Stand the dog away from you, clip downwards from the base of the tail towards the tip. Clip only about one-third of the tail to be sure to leave enough hair to create a glamorous pom-pom. Clip underneath the tail in the same way, being careful around the sensitive anus area.

CHOOSING A TRIM

TRADITIONAL LION CLIP

Rarely seen in the show ring today is the Full-Pack Traditional Lion Clip. This is hardly surprising in our busy world as this style takes far longer than any other in order to achieve excellence. It takes longer to dry, longer to groom and a lot longer to scissor than the Continental Lion. Where the result is achieved through clipping, the clipping is more difficult and the scissoring is artistically demanding. However, this is a beautiful trim for the show dog and looks especially spectacular on a white Standard Poodle.

It is always advisable to clip the mane in before the back end to make it easier to achieve good balance. Bath dog, clip feet, face, tail and stomach as for Puppy Trim. It is useful to have a photograph of a beautifully turned out Standard Poodle to copy from when first attempting this trim. Assuming you have shown your

FULL-PACK TRADITIONAL LION TRIM (BACK LEGS)
The front end is clipped first, using the same method for Traditional and Continenal Lion Trim.

  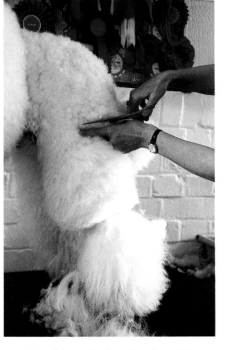

Marking the line to cut for Full-Pack Traditional Lion Trim – a bandage could be used for this.

Cutting line for the hock.

Marking the line for the stifle.

LEFT: Scissor to complete the trim.

RIGHT: The finished Full-Pack Traditional Lion Trim shown by Ch. Vanitonia Vivarita.

Photo: Carol Ann Johnson.

dog in Puppy Lion and have already an even parting around its middle, have the dog stand on the table and put a bandage around the front leg about two blade-lengths above the wrist joint. Cut round with scissors. From this bracelet line clip, with a number 10 to begin with, upwards to the elbow. Repeat for other front leg. Trim with scissors the bracelet to achieve an oval shape. Next trim with scissors the lower hair of the mane to form a ball appearance. This takes time and practice to achieve good results. Again, it is useful to have a photograph to copy from.

Now for the tricky part. Again I suggest you use a bandage (about one inch thick) to wrap around the hind leg at a point just above the hock, and at another point on the stifle joint. This will give you the appearance of what the shape will be once it is cut. You can move the bandage up or down a little to achieve a good balance. Cut an even, thin line, above the bandage, of hock and then the stifle. Use a 15 blade to clip these lines to about half-an-inch deep. No deeper, or you spoil the lines completely. Next turn the dog and repeat

on other leg. Check from the rear view that you have a uniform line across from one leg to the other before you cut the hair on the second leg. Comb hair upwards, allow the dog to shake itself, then tidy with scissors. The pack (over loin and hips) can be trimmed evenly to a length of about one inch. The bracelets of stifle and hock can be left a bit longer but try to achieve an even look from top to bottom. Remember, poetry-in-motion. This trim is far from being easy and takes a lot of practice to get right.

CONTINENTAL LION TRIM
This trim is loved by show people who have a dog with a fabulous back end that they want to show off, and the exhibitor who does not have so many free hours to spend preparing the Traditional Full-Pack Lion. It is, however, hated by most of the media and general public. Trim out front legs and scissor mane as for the Traditional Lion. Here, the back legs are shaved (with a number 10 blade to begin with, until the dog's skin has toughened, in which case you may use a 15 on some dogs, depending on the thickness of the coat) from just above the hock joint,

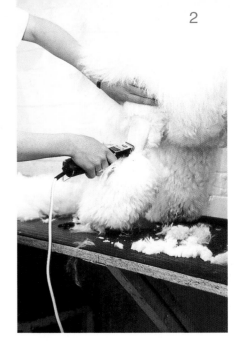

CONTINENTAL LION TRIM

1. Use scissors to mark the front bracelet.

2. Clip the hair from bracelet to elbow.

3. Scissor the bracelet.

4. Scissor round the bottom of the mane.

5. Brush the hindleg prior to styling.

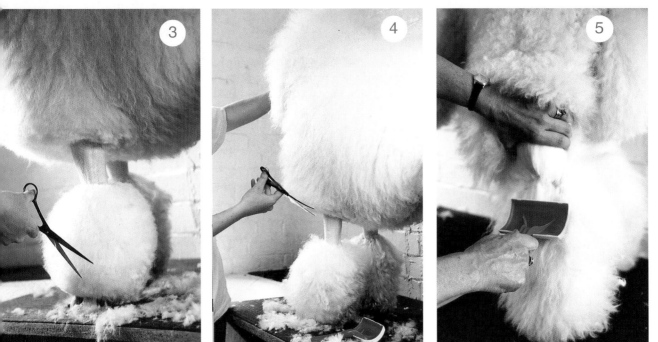

inside and out, to just above the stifle joint. Next, take a saucer and place the middle on the middle of the hip bone. Cut round the saucer with scissors. Now remove saucer to reveal a rosette over hip joint. Clip remaining hair off back legs, being careful not to clip into your newly-made rosette. Scissor the edges of the rosette to achieve a smart round puff.

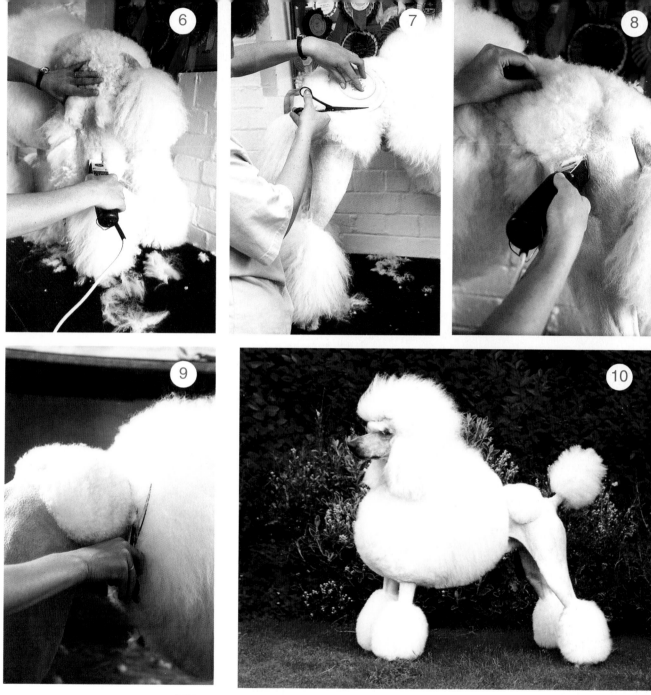

CONTINENTAL LION TRIM (BACK LEGS)

6. *Clip from hock to stifle for the Continental Lion Trim.*
7. *Use a saucer as a guide for cutting the rosette.*
8. *Clipping round the rosette.*
9. *Scissor the edge of the mane after the rosette has been tidied up.*
10. *The finished Continental Lion Trim.*

Lamb Trim: The most popular trim for pet owners.

LAMB TRIM

Sometimes called Curly Clip. This is the most popular style for the pet and companion Standard Poodle. Brush the coat thoroughly, bath and blow dry. See to ears and toe nail clipping as required. Shave feet, face and tail with 15 blade. Clip round the anal area rather than over it, but do be sure this area is clean. With a number 5 or 7 blade, clip down the back from the base of the head, just beneath the ears, clip neck on top and underneath, clip whole body, taking care to lift the front legs to clip under the arm, tightening loose skin at all times. And do take care when clipping over a bitch's teats, particularly when these are rather prominent. Clip down to the shoulder and to just below the hip bone. With a male you must gently protect the testicles with your hand while clipping the hair away from his private parts.

Now brush leg hair. Take up the scissors and trim the hair downwards as neatly as possible. Scissor in definite descent from top to bottom. Do not chop a bit from here, there and everywhere, or you will lose your silhouette line. Practice is essential. Scissoring does not come easily to most hairdressers. Trim hair from inside of legs keeping the scissors going in downward or upward strokes wherever possible. Do not cut crosswise unwisely, or you will finish with great gashes or chop marks. Scissor round the bottom of the leg hair, like putting the hem on the curtains. Trim back the top-knot, using scissors vertically to be sure to be safe around the eyes. Take care when scissoring the top-knot across the ears to make sure the leather is hanging down. Next, trim neatly across the back of the top-knot from ear to ear. The tail finishes the procedure. Hold the tip and comb hair outwards. Scissor round to form a ball or, as some people prefer, an oval shape. The more often you do this the easier the scissoring will become. And do not despair – we all make mistakes and cut bits of hair we did not mean to when the dog moves suddenly.

Sporting/Utility Trim: A good trim for the novice clipper.

SPORTING OR UTILITY CLIP

This trim is far easier for the beginner and most useful for a dog that leads an active life. Grooming procedure as for Lamb Trim. Clip feet, face and tail. Clip with number 5 or 7 the body as for Lamb, but now continue clipping down the whole front leg until just about a blade's length above the wrists. Clip down back leg, inside and out to the hock joint or just above. Leave too much rather than not enough hair, as you can always take more off if the balance does not look right for your individual dog. These remaining bracelets can be trimmed in an oval shape with the scissors. Trim top-knot and tail as for Lamb Trim.

DUTCH TRIM

Groom and clip feet, face and tail as with Lamb Trim. With clipper and number 10 blade, shave a line a blade's width between the shoulders right down to the base of the tail, clip abdomen from groin to navel and then downwards, incorporating the insides of the thighs. Clip the neck from below the ears to just above the shoulder. Brush leg hair upwards and scissor. This style is grossly unpopular today.

PUPPY TRIMS

The Puppy Trim is usually seen on puppies up to the age of nine months. However, most show people now clip their puppies into the Puppy Lion as young as five or six months. This latter trim was once only seen on puppies in the show ring. It was a style for puppies under the age of twelve months. In the show ring in most countries Standard Poodles are required to be trimmed into the traditional Lion Full-Pack or the Lion Continental. In Britain the Puppy Lion Trim is the most popular trim seen in the show ring today. With age, a more exaggerated version is achieved, which can hide faults from those judges who assess from glamour only. With the growth of the puppy coat, do be sure to put the top-knot up in pony-tail bands to

Dutch Trim: This trim needs a lot of on-going maintenance.

Puppy Trim: A popular trim with exhibitors.

prevent the hair from falling into the eyes. Streaming tears will result from neglect in this department.

THE FULL PUPPY TRIM

Bath and groom as normal, making sure to fluff-dry the coat completely. Clip feet, face and tail. Clip the tummy/abdomen from groin to navel and slightly down the inside of the hind legs with a number 10 blade. Comb the hair on the legs, then allow dog to shake itself. Trim with scissors around the hair at the bottom of the legs to allow a peep at the toes. Fluff up all body hair, then allow dog to shake itself again. Scissor to an even length all over body, including legs. As the coat grows in length, scissor slightly shorter from base of tail, blending the hair up towards the body to obtain an effective, easy-on-the-eye, shape.

PUPPY LION TRIM

This trim is not easily tackled by the novice trimmer as it requires hours of scissor work and needs an excellent eye to achieve a balanced and a poetic picture. However, it is lovely and is an exceedingly popular trim with exhibitors. Bath and groom dog. Clip feet, face and tail and abdomen as for Puppy Trim. Next, feel the body to ascertain last rib. If this is the first time you are attempting this trim, you could place a bandage around the body at just below this point to distinguish an even line. Cut hair with scissors held straight, up the edge of your line or bandage from the near side, up one side, over body and down the other side. You will probably find this much easier to do if the dog is standing square with its bottom towards you. Remove bandage, scissor the back legs to an even length rather like the back legs of the Lamb Trim. (Once you are well practised and have the eye to copy the up-to-date trimming you see in the show ring you can exaggerate the lines of this trim to suit and enhance your individual dog's needs.) Now you will need to blend the end of the mane. To do this, comb hair upwards and then allow to fall, scissor round to achieve a blend of the hair inclining towards the head to give the appearance of a long neck.

5 THE BREED STANDARDS

This chapter deals with the Breed Standards for the British Kennel Club (KC), the American Kennel Club (AKC), and the countries that come under the jurisdiction of the Fédération Cynologique International (FCI). The Breed Standard is set down to try to achieve a stability or foundation for the breed. Without a Breed Standard the breed could very quickly be endangered. It would be impossible to sustain a type. What some may see as an improvement may, in fact, be an exaggeration which could be detrimental if given a free hand. To understand a breed it is essential to read thoroughly, several times over, points of the breed. These should be studied before even the slightest consideration is given to breeding. And it is an essential part of the judge's, or prospective judge's, education and armoury fully to comprehend and to adhere to the Breed Standard. To newcomers of the breed these stipulations about points may seem boring and of little value, but if we look closely into these important requirements, we will see a picture begin to emerge. It is actually quite good fun to read each section of the British

Standard and compare it with the same section from the AKC and FCI Breed Standards, which in some cases are far more explicit than the KC version – and then see how some of your favourite dogs fare in comparison.

BRITISH BREED STANDARD

GENERAL APPEARANCE Well balanced, elegant looking with very proud carriage.

CHARACTERISTICS Distinguished by a special type of clip for show activity and by a coat which does not moult.

TEMPERAMENT Gay-spirited and good tempered.

HEAD AND SCULL Long and fine with slight peak. Scull not broad, moderate stop. Foreface strong, well chiselled, not falling away under eyes; cheek bones and muscle flat. Lips tight fitting. Chin defined but not protruding. Head in proportion to size of dog.

EYES Almond-shaped, dark, not set too close together, full of fire and intelligence.

EARS Leathers long and wide, set low, hanging close to face.

MOUTH Jaw strong with perfect, regular complete scissor bite, i.e. upper teeth closely overlapping lower teeth and set square to the jaw. A full set of 42 teeth is desirable.

NECK Well proportioned, of good length and strong to admit of the head being carried high and with dignity. Skin fitting tightly at the throat.

FOREQUARTERS Well laid back shoulders, strong and muscular. Legs set straight from shoulder, well muscled.

BODY Chest deep and moderately wide. Ribs well sprung and rounded. Back short, strong, slightly hollowed; loins broad and muscular.

HINDQUARTERS Thighs well developed and muscular; well bent stifles, hocks well let down; hindlegs turning neither in or out.

FEET Tight, proportionately small, oval in shape, turning neither in nor out, toes arched, pads thick and hard, well cushioned. Pasterns strong.

TAIL Set on rather high, carried at slight angle away from the body, never carried or curled over back, thick at root. Customarily docked.

GAIT/MOVEMENT Sound, free and light movement essential with plenty of drive.

COAT Very profuse and dense; of good harsh texture. All short hair close, thick and curly. It is strongly recommended that the traditional lion clip be adhered to.

COLOUR All solid colours. White and cream to have black nose, lips and eye rims, black toenails desirable. Brown to have dark amber eyes, dark liver nose, lips, eye rims and toenails. Apricot to have dark eyes with black points or deep amber eyes with liver points. Black, silver and blues to have black nose, lips, eye rims and toenails. Cream, apricot, browns, silver, and blues may show varying shades of the same colour up to 18 months. Clear colours preferred.

SIZE Poodles (Standard) over 38cm (15 inches)
     Poodles (Miniature) Height at shoulder should be under 38cm (15ins) but not under 28cm (11ins)
     Poodles (Toy) Height at shoulder should be under 28cm (11ins)

FAULTS Any departure from the foregoing points should be considered a fault and the seriousness with which the fault should be regarded should be in exact proportion to its degree.

NOTE Male animals should have two apparently normal testicles fully descended into the scrotum.

Reproduced by kind permission of the Kennel Club.

AMERICAN BREED STANDARD

The Standard for the Poodle (Toy variety) is the same as for the Standard and the Miniature varieties except as regard heights.

GENERAL APPEARANCE CARRIAGE AND CONDITION That of a very active, intelligent and elegant-appearing dog, squarely built, well proportioned, moving soundly and carrying himself proudly. Properly clipped in the traditional fashion and carefully groomed, the Poodle has about him an air of distinction and dignity peculiar to himself.

SIZE, PROPORTION, SUBSTANCE
Size: The Standard Poodle is over 15 inches at the highest point of the shoulders. Any Poodle which is 15 inches or less in height shall be disqualified from competition as a Standard Poodle.
The Miniature Poodle is 15 inches at the highest point of the shoulders, with a minimum height in excess of 11 inches. Any Poodle which is over 15 inches or is 11 inches or less at the highest point of the shoulders shall be disqualified as a Miniature Poodle.
The Toy Poodle is 11 inches or under at the highest point of the shoulders. Any Poodle which is more than 11 inches at the highest point of the shoulders shall be disqualified from competition as a Toy Poodle.
As long as the Toy Poodle is definitely a Toy Poodle, and the Miniature a Miniature Poodle, both in balance and proportion for the variety, diminutives shall be the deciding factor when all other points are equal.
Proportion: To insure the desirable squarely built appearance, the length of body measured from the breastbone to the point of the rump approximates the height from the highest point of the shoulders to the ground.
Substance: Bone and muscle of both forelegs and hindlegs are in proportion to size of dog.

HEAD AND EXPRESSION (a) Eyes: very dark, oval in shape and set far enough apart and positioned to create an alert intelligent expression. Major fault; eyes round, protruding, large or very light.
(b) Ears: hanging close to the head, set at or slightly below eye level. The ear leather is long, wide and thickly feathered; however, the ear fringes should not be of excessive length.
(c) Scull: moderately rounded, with a slight but definite stop. Cheekbones and muscles flat. Length from occiput to stop about the same length as muzzle.
(d) Muzzle: long, straight and fine, with slight chiselling under the eyes. Strong without lippiness. The chin definite enough to preclude snipiness. Major fault: lack of chin.
Teeth white, strong, and with a scissor bite. Major fault: undershot, overshot, wry mouth.

NECK, TOPLINE, BODY Neck well proportioned, strong and long enough to permit the head to be carried high and with dignity. Skin snug at throat. The neck rises from strong, smoothly muscled shoulders. Major fault: ewe neck.
The topline is level, neither sloping nor roached, from the highest point of the shoulder blade to the base of the tail, with the exception of a slight hollow just behind the shoulder.
Body (a) Chest deep and moderately wide with well sprung ribs.
(b) The loin is short, broad and muscular.
(c) Tail straight, set on high and carried up, docked, of sufficient length to insure a balanced outline. Major fault: set low, curled, or carried over the back.

FOREQUARTERS Strong, smoothly muscled shoulders. The shoulder blade is well laid back and approximately the same length as the upper foreleg. Major fault: steep shoulder.
(a) Forelegs straight and parallel when viewed from the front. When viewed from the side the elbow is directly below the highest point of the shoulder. The pasterns are strong. Dewclaws may be removed.

FEET The feet are rather small, oval in shape with toes well arched and cushioned on thick firm pads. Nails short but not excessively shortened. The feet turn neither in nor out. Major fault: paper or splay foot.

HINDQUARTERS The angulation of the hindquarters balances that of the forequarters. (a) Hind legs straight and parallel when viewed from the rear. Muscular with width in the region of the stifles which are well bent; femur and tibia are about equal in length; hock to heel short and perpendicular to the ground. When standing, the rear toes are only slightly behind the point of the rump. Major fault: cow-hocks.

COAT (a) Quality: (1) Curly: of natural harsh texture, dense throughout. (2) Corded: hanging in tight even cords of varying length; longer on mane or body coat, head, and ears; shorter on puffs, bracelets, and pompoms.
(b) Clip: A Poodle under 12 months may be shown in the 'Puppy' clip. In all regular classes, Poodles 12 months or over must be shown in the 'English Saddle' or 'Continental' clip. In the Stud Dog and Brood Bitch classes and in non-competitive Parade of Champions, Poodles may be shown in the 'Sporting' clip. A Poodle in any other type of clip shall be disqualified.
(1) 'Puppy': A Poodle under a year old may be shown in the 'Puppy' clip with the coat long. The face, throat, feet and base of tail are shaved. The entire shaven foot is visible, there is a pom-pom on the end of the tail. In order to give a neat appearance and a smooth unbroken line, shaping of the coat is permissible.
(2) 'English Saddle': In the 'English Saddle' clip the face, throat, feet, forelegs and base of tail are shaved, leaving puffs on the forelegs and a pom-pom on the end of the tail. The hindquarters are covered with a short blanket of hair except for a curved shaved area on each flank and two shaven bands on each hindleg. The entire body is left in full coat but may be shaped in order to ensure overall balance.
(3) 'Continental': In the 'Continental' clip, the face, throat, feet, and base of tail are shaved. The hindquarters are shaved with pompoms (optional) on the hips. The legs are shaved, leaving bracelets on the hindlegs and puffs on the forelegs. There is a pompom on the end of the tail. The entire shaven foot and a portion of the shaven foreleg above the puff are visible. The rest of the body is left in full coat but may be shaped in order to insure overall balance.
(4) 'Sporting': In the 'Sporting' clip, a Poodle shall be shown with face, feet, throat, and base of tail shaved, leaving a scissored cap on the top of the head and a pompom on the end of the tail. The rest of the body, and legs are clipped or scissored to follow the outline of the dog leaving a short blanket of coat no longer than one inch in length. The hair on the legs may be slightly longer than that on the body.

In all clips the hair of the topknot may be left free or held in place by elastic bands. The hair is only of sufficient length to present a smooth outline. 'Topknot' refers only to hair on the skull, from stop to occiput. This is the only area where elastic bands may be used.

COLOR All solid colors: The coat is an even and solid color at the skin. In creams, apricots, browns, silvers and blues the coat may show varying shades of the same color, as is frequently present in the somewhat darker feathering of the ears, and the tipping of the ruff. While clear colors are definitely preferred, such natural variation in the shading should not be considered a fault.
Whites and creams to have black nose, lips and eyerims, black toenails desirable; browns to have dark amber eyes, dark liver nose, lips and toenails; apricots to have dark eyes with black points or deep amber eyes with liver points; blacks, silvers and blues to have black nose, lips and eyerims and toenails.

GAIT A straightforward trot with light springy action and strong hindquarters drive. Head and tail carried up. Sound effortless movement is essential.

TEMPERAMENT Carrying himself proudly, very active, intelligent, the Poodle has an air of distinction and dignity peculiar to himself. Major fault: shyness or sharpness.

MAJOR FAULTS Any distinct deviation from the declared characteristics described in the Breed Standard.

DISQUALIFICATIONS Size. A dog over or under the height limits specified shall be disqualified.

Clip: A dog in any type of clip other than those listed under coat shall be disqualified.
Parti-colours: The coat of a parti-coloured dog is not an even solid colour at the skin but two or more colours. Parti-coloured dogs shall be disqualified.

VALUE OF POINTS

General appearance, temperament, carriage and condition	30
Head, expression, ears, eyes and teeth	20
Body, neck, legs, feet and tail	20
Gait	20
Coat, color and texture	10

Reproduced by kind permission of the American Kennel Club.

FÉDÉRATION CYNOLOGIQUE INTERNATIONALE (FCI) STANDARD

GENERAL APPEARANCE AND CHARACTERISTICS Characterisation of the Breed. The Poodle is classified as a companion dog, of harmonious appearance with the characteristically wavy or corded coat clipped in the traditional fashion. The general impression is that of an intelligent animal, always alert, active, harmoniously built, elegant in appearance, and carrying himself proudly. The Poodle has a light, springy gait, which should never be stretched or far reaching. His faithfulness and willingness to learn and to be trained make the Poodle a particularly pleasant companion.

HEAD The head is distinguished, with straight lines, and its size is in correct proportion to the body. The length of the head should be slightly more than

2/5 of the dog's height at the withers. It should neither be too heavy and coarse, nor too pointed.

NOSE Well developed and pronounced; well chiselled with recognisable features under the covering skin; when viewed in profile the nasal bridge extends in an almost vertical line, nostrils well open. Black, white and silver Poodles have a black nose, brown Poodles a brown nose; all other colours from dark brown to black, without preferring the black colour; however, a black nose is acceptable for the apricot Poodle in order to prevent loss of pigmentation.

MUZZLE Strong, elegant, yet not pointed, with a straight upper profile. The length should be about 9/10 of the head. The two lower jaws run almost parallel to each other. The muzzle is strong and noble; but not pointed. Its lower profile is determined by the bones of the lower jaw not the edges of the lips.

LIPS Well-formed, dry, of medium thickness. The lower lips are well fitting and the upper lips meet the lower lips without overlapping. The colour should be black for black, white and silver Poodles; and brown for brown Poodles; all other colours from dark brown to black, without preferring the black colour, yet it is accepted for the apricot Poodle in order to prevent loss of pigmentation.

JAWS Well fitting with strong teeth.

CHEEKS The muscles lie flat on the cheekbones. The curvature under the eye sockets must be well chiselled and only slightly filled. The masseter muscles, as an anatomical basis of the cheeks, should not be strongly developed, the eyebrows only slightly protruding.

STOP Slight stop.

SKULL Well formed. Its width is less than half the length of the head. (The longitudinal axis of the skull forms, together with the sidelines of the face, an angle of 16 to 19 degrees.) Eyebrows are slightly protruding, covered with long hair. The head, lengthways, viewed from above, appears oval with a slight curve. The sidelines of the face taper gently.

FURROW BETWEEN BROWS Broad between the eyes, lessens towards the well pronounced occiput. (Occiput is somewhat less pronounced in Toy Poodles.)

EYES Fiery expression. The eyes are set at the level of the stop, and are slightly oblique. The shape of the eyelids gives the eyes the almond shape. Black or dark brown eye colour for black, white, silver and apricot Poodles, for brown Poodles the eyes must be of a dark amber colour.

EARS Quite long, extending beyond the cheeks; the base of the ear starts at an extended imaginary line drawn from the nose to the outer corner of the eye. The ears hang close and flat to the head and have rounded lower edges. They are covered with very long hair. A Poodle whose ear leather does not reach the corners of the mouth, may not be rated excellent.

NECK Firm with slight arch of the nape, of medium length and well-proportioned, without dewlap. Head carried high and with dignity. The neck must be oval in diameter, its length is shorter than the length of the head.

FOREQUARTERS Shoulder and upper arm: Withers not too pronounced; sloping, well-muscled shoulder blades. The shoulder blade and upper arm form an angle of approximately 90 to 110 degrees. The length of the upper arm is approximately the same as that of the shoulder blade.

FORELEGS Straight, parallel, well-muscled with firm bones. Measured from the ground, the height of the elbow is about 5/9 of the dog's height at the withers.

PASTERN JOINT In a straight extended line with the foreleg.

PASTERN Strong, not plump, viewed from the side almost straight.

FEET Small, compact, short and oval. The toes are well arched, strong, with skin between the toes, standing vertically in the hard, thick pads. The nails of the black and silver Poodles are black; those of the brown Poodles are black or brown; those of the white Poodle may be dark or lighter; however, they must correspond to the pigmentation. White nails are faulty. The nails of the apricot Poodle must be in the colour ranges of dark brown, towards black; although the black colour is not preferred, it is acceptable.

BODY Well proportioned. The length of the body should be somewhat longer than the dog's height at the withers.

FORECHEST Normal as in similarly structured breeds. The prosternum

protrudes slightly and is situated rather high, resulting in a higher, lighter and more elegant carriage of the head.

CHEST The width of the chest at the elbow is 2/3 of its height (from the withers to the sternum). The chest circumference, measured behind the shoulder, must exceed the height of the withers by at least 10cm.

RIBS Rib cage oval, broad in the area of the back.

BACK Harmonious and short. Neither with a roach nor a dip in the back. The height from the ground to the withers is almost the same as the height from the ground to the croup.

LOINS Firm and well-muscled.

BELLY AND FLANKS Tucked up (without giving a greyhound-like appearance).

CROUP Rounded, but not sloping.

TAIL Set rather high, at loin level. It should be docked to 1/3 to 1/2 of its natural length, but may be left at its full length for the corded Poodle. A long, well-carried tail is not faulty in this case and while the dog is in motion, it is carried at a slanted angle.

HINDQUARTERS Upper Thigh: The hind legs, as viewed from the rear, are parallel, very muscular and strongly developed, forming an almost right angle at the stifle. The pelvis and the upper thigh, the upper thigh and lower thigh, and the lower thigh and the hocks should be sufficiently angulated so as to prevent the dog from having a undesirable sloping croup.

HOCK JOINTS AND HOCK Vertical, without dewclaws.

FEET See front feet.

COAT Colour: For the 'Wool' and the 'Corded' Poodles: black, brown, silver, white and apricot.
(a) The brown colour should have a strong tone, should be sufficiently dark, uniform in colour and warm. The shade of the brown colour may not be close to beige or even lighter than beige. The dark brown colour may not be close to black, as seen in the 'tête de nègre' or the 'aubergine'.
(b) The silver colour must be uniform and may not show traces of black or white.
(c) The apricot colour must be uniform, it may neither have a tendency towards the beige, cream, or brown colours and their nuances.
CLIP (a) 'Lion Clip': The wool and the corded Poodles are clipped at the hindquarters up to the ribs. Also clipped, the top and bottom part of the muzzle starting from the lower eyelids, cheeks, the front and hind legs, leaving bracelets on the hindlegs and puffs on the forelegs and the optional pompoms on the hindquarters; the tail is shaved except for a round, oblong pompom at the tip. Leaving moustaches is recommended, trousers may be left on the forelegs.
(b) 'Modern Clip': In this clip, the hair may be left on all four legs, provided the following rules are specifically followed. The following will be clipped: (a) The lower part of the front legs from the nails to the dewclaw; the lower part of the hindleg to the same height as the front legs. Machine clipping is permitted provided it is limited to the toes. (b) The head and tail will be clipped the same as in the Lion Clip. In this style of clip the following exceptions are allowed: (1) The presence of short hair beneath the lower jaw, not surpassing: however, the length of 1cm with the lower line (profile) cut parallel to the jaw (the so-called 'goat's beard' is not acceptable) (2) Absence of the pompom on the tail (this will, however, slightly diminish the rating for coat texture).
'Corded Poodle'. Abundant hair of woolly texture forming the characteristic cords of even length. These should be at least 20cm long. The longer the better. The cords on both sides of the head, above the ears, may be tied together with a hairband; the others should be arranged to the left and right of the body to give a groomed appearance.

SKIN The pigmentation of the black, brown, silver, and apricot Poodles must be in accordance with their coat colour. For white Poodles a silver-coloured skin is highly desirable; however, the pigmentation should not affect the colour of the woolly coat. There are also some white Poodles with a very light (pink) skin and pigmented spots, not only on the underside but also on other parts of the body. This is not a fault. The overall pigmentation and its intensity is particularly important at the eyelids, nose, lips, gums, oral tissues, vulva, the vent, testicles and pads. It must be black for black Poodles, white and silver Poodles, dark brown for brown Poodles. For apricot Poodles it must be uniform in colour and as dark as possible in the shades of dark brown to blackish, without particularly preferring the blackish colour; however, it is acceptable in the apricot Poodle in order to avoid a loss of pigmentation.

SIZE Standard Poodle 45 to 58cm.

ANATOMICAL FAULTS AND FAULTS OF TYPE Muzzle too narrow or too pointed. Roman nose. Small, insufficiently open or too large a nose. Missing stop or too much stop. Eyes too small or too large, insufficiently dark or shimmering red. Ears too short, too narrow or carried backward. Overshot is a fault which must be judged according to its seriousness. Distempered yellow teeth are not a fault if positioned correctly. Badly positioned or missing teeth will be judged according to its seriousness. Canines and molars cannot be missing. One missing P-1 is not a fault. An 'excellent' may still be awarded for two missing P-1s. A 'very good' may be awarded for three missing premolars (three P-1s or two P-1s and one P-2). Sloping croup, steep rear angulation, high on the legs; tail bent towards the back or low set tail. Floating or too far-reaching gait. Light nose with insufficient pigmentation, spotted nose. Pigmentation spots, insufficient overall pigmentation, depigmentation at the eyelids, spectacle effect, or lack of hair around the eyes. Insufficient, soft coat. Colour indefinite or not uniform. Some single white hairs at the chest may be tolerated. Meanness, aggression, or overtly nervous dogs. Poodles of 'dwarf-like' appearance may not be rated 'excellent'. The obvious signs therefore are: head too round, missing indentation at forehead, too much stop, protruding eyes, forehead too pointed, too short or coarse hair, receding lower jaw, missing chin.

DISQUALIFYING FAULTS White spots, white hair at feet, parti-coloured Poodles, monorchids and cryptorchids. Dewclaws or traces of dewclaws at rear legs. Undershot. Poodles higher in size than 60cm or lower than 26cm. Poodles which are not in the proper show clip may not be recommended for awards or rated during shows; however, they may be used for breeding.

NOTE Male animals should have two apparently normal testicles fully descended into the scrotum.

Reproduced by kind permission of the Fédération Cynologique Internationale. Translated into English by Mrs Kincaid.

INTERPRETING THE BREED STANDARDS

GENERAL APPEARANCE
To many Poodle judges 'attitude' is one of the most important aspects of our breed. This means that the Poodle has an outgoing character, is active and proud and can move elegantly with a well-balanced gait. The words 'poetry-in-motion' I think sum up rather well the 'attitude' required in the Poodle.

CHARACTERISTICS
Probably the most distinctive characteristic of the Poodle is its coat, which is quite different to any other dogs in existence. There may be breeds with similar coats, such as the Irish Water Spaniel, but none with such distinction as the Poodle. The curly wool that does not moult is its special feature. The coat must always be clean and thoroughly groomed.

TEMPERAMENT
A happy dog which is kind, willing to please and extremely faithful to friends,

Line drawings:
Viv Rainsbury.

The Standard Poodle:
Correct proportions.

easy to train and wonderful to live with –
the very best companion. There is no
excuse for breeding from a dog or bitch
whose temperament is not absolutely
typical Poodle. They are fun-loving dogs
whose attitude is completely amenable.

THE SKELETON
The skeleton of the Standard Poodle
shows a well-balanced dog. Regardless of
whether the dog is long in body, long in
leg, ultra-short in body, short-legged,
heavy, lacking in substance, slab-sided,
over-angulated, or whatever, the dog will
have the same number of bones. The
Poodle Breed Standards call for a back
which is short, and this has caused some
confusion. I have seen a picture of a
skeleton shortened in the loin by two
vertebrae. This is impossible. At the end
of the day the Poodle will have the basic
bone structure of any dog. They cannot
have fewer bones because we choose to
like them short in the back. In fact, in all

the Breed Standards for the Poodle it
states that the 'back' is short; of the 'loin'
they say; broad and muscular, or firm
and muscular, and yet, strangely it is the
loin that is shortened in diagrams and
not the actual five bones of the back.

Let us run through the bones present
in all dogs and their forefathers – wolves.
Starting from the top, (see Page 80), we
have:
1) Skull fitted to neck by ball and socket
joint. 2) Pole joint behind the first two
vertebrae. 3) Seven vertebrae of the neck.
4) Eight vertebrae of the withers. 5) Five
vertebrae of the back. 6) Seven vertebrae
of the loin. 7) Three fused vertebrae of
the croup. 8) Vertebrae of the tail
depending on dock. 9) One pair of
floating ribs. 10) Three pairs of asternal
ribs joining each other at base. 11) Nine
sternal ribs. 12) Sternum. The
appendicular consists of 13) Shoulder
blade/scapula. 14) Shoulder point(which
is a ball and socket joint). 15) The upper

The skeleton.

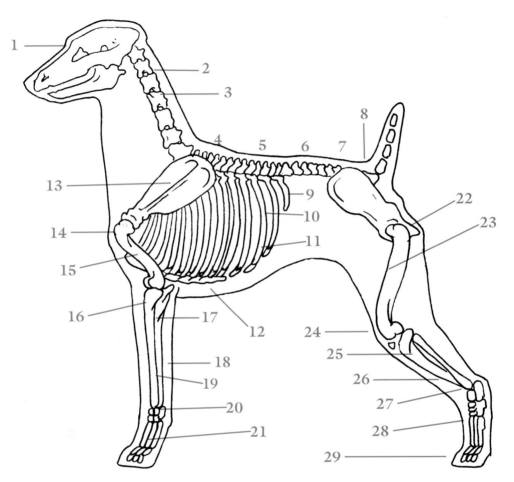

arm/humerus. 16) Elbow. 17) Fore arm/radius and ulna. 18) Pisiform. 19) Pastern joint consisting of seven bones. 20) Five metacarpals of pastern. 21) Phalanges of the four toes. 22) Pelvis. 23) Upper thigh/femur. 24) Knee cap/patella. 25) Lower thigh/tibia and fibia. 26) Os Calcis. 27) Five metatarsal bones forming hock. 29) Phalanges of toes. On each leg one metacarpal is the dewclaw positioned on the inside of the leg and removed when found on Poodles.

HEAD AND SKULL

Although called for to be long and fine in head, this does sometimes become open to misinterpretation. It must never be forgotten that the Poodle was first used as a working/retrieving/water dog. It carried birds and ducks in its mouth. If the muzzle or head is exaggerated and is too long and fine, this is in direct opposition to the origin of the breed. The foreface is required to be strong and well-chiselled and not falling away under the eyes. Heads that are too fine are in strict deviance from this requirement. The skull should not be so broad that the impression is of a clumsy, big head. A Poodle should always look attractive and well-balanced in head. For balance, it is essential to look at the dog as a whole. A tiny head on a very large dog is totally out of balance. A harmonious picture will be a balanced one.

Heads are the all-important object to some judges. We all feel attracted to a nice face, but that is not enough. In future years we want our Poodles to still be capable of functioning in the wide spectrum of activities they enjoy today. If we, as judges, choose to forget the true ancestral function of our breed we will lose its qualities. Show dogs may well be

The foreface is strong and well-chiselled.

*A well-balanced head creates
a harmonious picture.*

THE HEAD

Correct proportions.

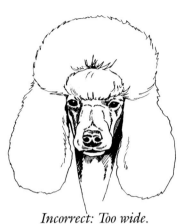

Incorrect: Too wide.

Incorrect: Too short.

glamorous – we do not want it any other way but what we require equally is a Poodle retaining its wonderful gay-spirited temperament and sound free movement. Without these virtues a beautiful face is useless. The whole dog should be seriously considered when judging, and not just one part.

EYES
Imagine an almond nut. Crack open an almond and look closely at the nut. This is the shape required and sought after.

Dark eyes are a point deemed necessary, but expression is also desired, and to achieve good expression the eye is not always deeply dark. Darkish brown is fairly well accepted. Eye colour does depend on the colour of the coat. The main requirement is that the eye should be as close to the Standard as possible, with an alert, full-of-life expression.

EARS
A Standard Poodle with short, thin ears, or ears that fly when it is standing still

THE EYES

Correct almond-shaped eyes.

Incorrect: Round eyes.

Incorrect: Small, squinty eyes.

THE EARS

Correct: Long, wide ears hanging close to the head.

Incorrect: Too small.

Incorrect: High-set and flying.

and not racing in the wind is not typical. Ear leathers need to be at least as long as the nose, and are usually brought forward to be measured against the nose by judges. The leather should be wide, and hanging close to the face.

MOUTH
The jaws are to be strong, with enough width to allow for a full set of forty-two teeth. It is not the end of the world if a dog has a missing tooth, but all breeders should strive to maintain a full set with the required scissor bite. The bite, as shown, is extremely important and no show dog will win with either an overshot or an undershot mouth.

NECK
Well proportioned, of good length, strong with tight-fitting skin. Dewlaps and loose rolls of skin are ugly on a Poodle and will not be accepted. The neck needs to be long enough to give the

THE MOUTH

Correct scissor bite.

Incorrect: Undershot.

Incorrect: Overshot.

grace required in this breed. Again, balance is important. One cannot expect a small dog to have the same length of neck as a large dog. The proportions should be right, to give the appearance of a Poodle with becoming elegance of carriage. This is not achieved with a neck that is short.

FOREQUARTERS

The shoulders on a Poodle are laid well back. An upright shoulder will give the appearance of a short neck, so it is fairly easy to spot. The trimmer who is not as clever as some can leave too much hair on the back and make the neck appear short. It is always wise for a novice judge to feel several dogs with an expert, and discuss this issue. In time it is easy to spot at a glance if the appearance of a short neck is due to incorrect angulation or incorrect trimming. The front legs of the Poodle should be set straight from the shoulder. From the side the front feet should stand beneath the point of the shoulder, giving the appearance of a straight line running through from top to bottom. Feet face forward and do not turn in nor out. Having said that, some of the larger Poodles do take a little more time than the smaller ones to develop,

and may be slightly lazy in the front stance until they are, perhaps, 13 to 14 months old. Judges must take this into consideration.

Front assembly does cause some confusion. In the skeleton we see a balanced front. The shoulder slopes well back as closely to 45 degrees as possible. This lay-back can only be accurately assessed when the dog is standing with its heel-pad in a direct line with the centre of the shoulder – the centre of the shoulder being where the shoulder pivots, the centre of the blade. If we stand the dog with its front heel pads further forward, this will thrust the shoulder blade back, giving a false impression of lay-back of shoulder.

When we come to the upper arm, the humerus, the more slender bone which runs from the shoulder blade backwards to join the forearm, we have an interesting variance in the three different Breed Standards. The English version does not mention an upper arm; though I am quite sure all English Poodles do have a humerus! We see in the FCI Standard that the shoulder blade and the upper arm form an angle of approximately 90 to 110 degrees, the length of the bones being the same. The

FOREQUARTERS

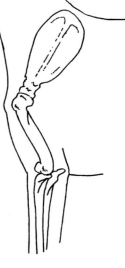

Correct front angulation.

Incorrect: Too upright.

Correct front.

Incorrect: Too wide.

Incorrect: Too narrow.

American Breed Standard is much the same as the English, except that it states that the shoulder blade and upper arm are approximately the same length.

Correct front angulation will result in correct head carriage. When judging, it is perhaps wise to discover whether a dog is poking its head forward because it is badly angulated or whether it is tired or resting. Watch a working horse when it is out on a road exercising programme to build muscle. Its head is carried well forward and only lifts when it is trotting, or collected; very fast movement and galloping will result in the head coming back down. Watch Poodles moving at different speeds and notice the difference in head carriage. This will apply no matter what degree of angulation is found. Ride a horse with straight shoulders and you feel the bumps shaking your whole body. Ride one with a good front assembly and you will not be able to believe the difference in the smooth, even, comfortable ease in which you cover the ground. The Poodle Breed Standard calls for light springy gait – sound free and light movement – a straightforward trot with light, springy action. The Poodle does not have a stretched, far-reaching action or gait. The Poodle should be poetry-in-motion. No dog can move with such a pleasing effect unless it is correctly constructed. If a dog you are judging cannot move freely forward, ask yourself why not. It may not be your job to decide why the dog has problems, but you must be capable of recognising unsoundness.

BODY
The body of the Standard Poodle should not in any way give the impression of weediness or weakness. The chest should be deep and wide enough to give the appearance of a dog able to move with agility, and of substance without clumsiness. When feeling the Poodle's chest, the prosternum should appear obvious and is high in order to achieve elegant carriage. There is a slight hollow behind the withers, but not so deep as to cause weakness. Any roachness here is uncharacteristic and undesired. The body, as with all the other points, should have good muscular quality.

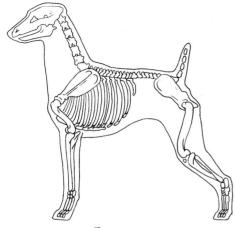

Correct structure.

Incorrect: The bone structure and number of bones does not vary, but for a Standard Poodle, this dog is too long in the back.

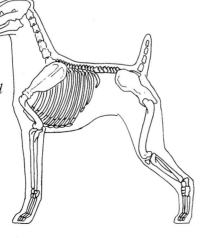

Incorrect: This dog is not balanced as it is too short in the back and too long in the leg. Again the bone structure and number of bones remain the same.

The chest and rib cage of the Poodle is deep and well-sprung and rounded – oval, broad in the area of the back – chest deep and moderately wide with well sprung ribs. Because the Poodle is a fine dog we sometimes see judges putting up dogs with the finest head and finest body. There is little substance in this body. Equally we do not want the thickset, more cobby front of the Labrador. What we are looking for in the Poodle is that balance which gives us width between the front legs at the elbow from a well-sprung rib. The FCI Standard calls for the width of chest at the elbow to be 2/3 of its height (from the wither to the sternum).

HINDQUARTERS
To move in a harmonious, balanced way, a Poodle must have hindquarters to complement the front end, otherwise the movement will fall short, or the Poodle will overreach. The quarters of the Poodle should not be exaggerated as this will cause weakness. A Poodle should be capable of running, jumping and thoroughly enjoying itself. It cannot do this where the quarters are weak, lack muscle and are not well balanced. The stifle, or knee joint, is required to be well bent, but this does not mean the knees should be close to the ground. The hind legs should both be set looking ahead, turning neither inwards nor outwards. The hocks are set low. You could say that if the Poodle is not proportionally set right, it will have a tail which is too high set, or too low set.

The hindquarters of the Poodle incorporate the croup, but only in the FCI Breed Standard is the croup mentioned: rounded, but not sloping. The pelvis and upper thigh (femur), the upper thigh and lower thigh (tibia and

HINDQUARTERS

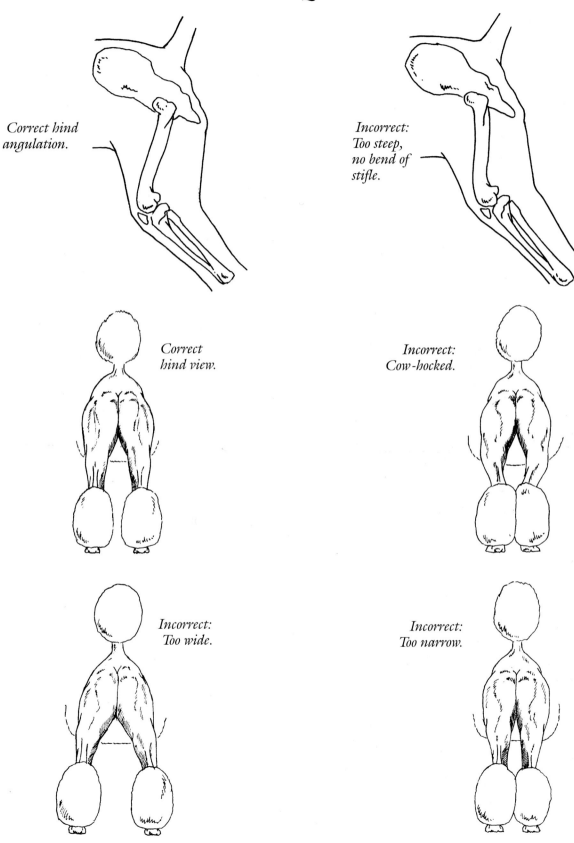

Correct hind
angulation.

Incorrect:
Too steep,
no bend of
stifle.

Correct
hind view.

Incorrect:
Cow-hocked.

Incorrect:
Too wide.

Incorrect:
Too narrow.

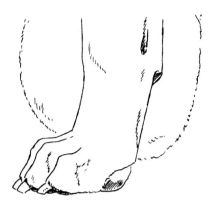

Correct oval feet.

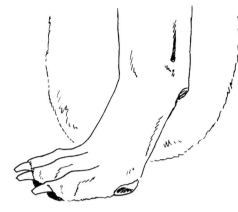

Incorrect: Flat and weak.

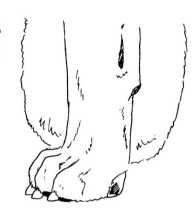

Incorrect: Round, 'cat' foot.

fibia), and the lower thigh and the hocks should be sufficiently angulated to prevent the dog from having an undesirable sloping croup. The English version gives us thighs well developed and muscular, well bent stifles, hocks well let down, hindlegs turning neither in nor out. The American Standard is roughly similar.

A Poodle can be too steep in the croup as well as too flat. The 30 degree slope of the pelvis, with the dog static, gives us the advantage of a well-balanced rear capable of work or ease of movement. The angulation of the pelvis is revealed in the outline of the Poodle. Beauty trimming in today's current fashion of heavily-coated rear ends can easily alter the visual effect of the pelvis. Of course, judges that know their stuff will soon discover this variance. The high-set tail which is called for (totally different to the 'gay tail' which is carried over the back) is achieved by the degree of the croup. With the pelvis sloping too far down we see a lower-set tail. If the pelvis is very high, a flat croup will result, and with it the tail that is carried over the back from its root.

FEET

The feet are an extremely important part of the anatomy, giving strength for mobility and neatness to complete a picture of overall quality. The feet should be fairly small and look neat and compact. They should be oval in shape and the toes should be well-arched; the underpart or pads should be thick and well-cushioned. Remember, the Standard Poodle is a performance breed, and activity will be restrained where feet are of poor quality. The most unattractive fault is long, open-toed feet which give insufficient strength. Other faults are splayed feet or thin, flat feet. Poorly constructed feet cannot be improved by exercise. However, well-formed feet will tighten with exercise, improving their general appearance.

THE TAIL

Although in the Breed Standard it is stated that the tail should be set on rather high, this does in no way excuse breeders for ignoring bad tail carriage. The tail of a stud dog feeling frisky may well be rather forward, or an overlong tail may be banana-shaped. The tail

TAIL

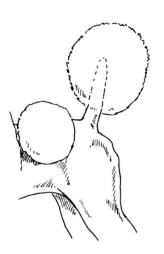 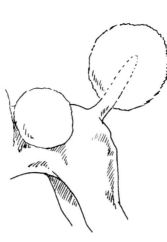 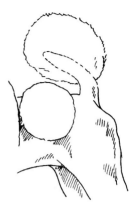

Correct tail-set.   *Incorrect: Too low.*   *Incorrect: Curled over back.*

should never be curled or carried over the back like a Spitz breed. This is most uncharacteristic. Handlers that try to push the tail over the back towards the shoulder are attempting to make the dog look shorter. They are totally ignoring the Breed Standard. The tail in itself might cause confusion when left undocked. The length will often produce a banana effect. Still the tail should be carried away from the body at the base and never be over the back. As previously stated, the set of the croup will determine tail carriage from the body.

GAIT AND MOVEMENT
Look for that balance, that poetry-in-motion. A light, springy action that flows forward without jolting up and down. Not too far stretched or reaching and not short and stilted.

MOVEMENT

TOP LEFT: *Correct light and springy action.*

ABOVE: *Incorrect: Over-reaching.*

LEFT: *Incorrect: Pacing.*

6 *THE SHOW RING*

Showing dogs can be great fun. Provided your dog is pure-bred and is registered with the appropriate governing body, it qualifies for showing. Some of us with the drive and enthusiasm, and yes, a sort of madness about us, travel hundreds of miles, often each week, in order to spend a few minutes running round a ring so that our dogs can compete against others – and the day before the show we will spend several hours shampooing, clipping and scissoring our Standard Poodles in preparation for this.

MAKING THE DECISION

You may be the proud owner of a beautiful Standard Poodle. Perhaps friends, and those you meet out walking, stop to admire your elegant pet. They impress upon you that the dog ought to be shown. Well, should it? Showing is a fascinating and rewarding hobby, though never financially so. And, who knows, you may be the owner of a potential winner. So, should you show your Standard Poodle? His father is a World Champion of Crufts! – a title that does not exist. Your dog comes from the top

breeder! – there is no such person. Your dog is perfect! – impossible.

Dog shows are fun but they can also be frustrating. Not all judges are as wise as we would like them to be. Not all exhibitors are as perfect as we would like them to be. Dog showing requires serious consideration by a pet owner before they jump in feet first. Provided you keep it in mind that no matter if the judge prefers the black, whose head you dislike, more than your beautifully headed blue, because the judge is either colour prejudiced or blind (our usual excuse when we feel sad because our beloved pet has been beaten) – at the end of the day your pet is the same loveable friend, companion, and wonderful Standard Poodle as he was before the show. Remember that, and you will fare well. f you have been to a few shows, have developed an interest, have shown your pet to a few judges at ring training classes, have sought the opinion of the breeder on the dog's creditability, and have been given sound advice to go ahead and show, then do so. Choose your shows carefully to suit your needs and pocket, and above all, enjoy yourself.

Keep it light, meet some lovely people and know a new and entertaining social life. With average luck you may do nicely. You may find, like the rest of us 'mad dog folk', that all the trials and tribulations are worth it in the long run.

SHOWS IN THE UK
CHAMPIONSHIP SHOWS are where the greatest number of quality Standard Poodles are seen. These shows are quite pressurised and time-consuming as they are usually hundreds of miles away, and they are jolly hard work as well as being the most expensive shows to enter. Standard Poodle classes at All Breed Championship shows, as well as at the Breed Club Championship Shows, always attract large entries. The standard of handling is high at this level of showing, making the competition fierce. Classes vary through ages such as: Minor Puppy 6-9 months; Puppy 6-12 months; Junior 12-18 months; with Maiden (for dogs never having won a first prize) and Novice (for dogs not having won three first prizes); then on to Post Graduate (for dogs not having won four first prizes), Post Graduate (for dogs not having won five first prizes, Limit (for dogs not having won seven first prizes), and Open (open to all). The same classes are offered for the bitches.

The best bitch and the best dog compete for Best of Breed. At most Championship shows there are, on offer, a Challenge Certificate (CC) for the male and one for the female. To win a CC a dog of either sex must beat all dogs of the same sex, including Champions, which are invariably entered in the Open Class. There is also a Reserve Challenge Certificate (Res. CC) for the runner-up of each sex. For the novice exhibitor, or for young puppies, it is less stressful to begin at the Open show level.

Shiremica All A Dream, pictured at ten months: Showing a Standard Poodle is hard work, but it can be very rewarding.

OPEN SHOWS are a lot less competitive and it is relatively easy to find one placed in a venue much closer to home. One cannot make a Champion at this level. When you consider how few of the Standard Poodles shown in the UK each year come anywhere near this status you will see showing in its right perspective.

Open shows are considerably cheaper to enter. Many exhibitors prefer to stay at the Open level, but if one owns a really nice specimen of the breed, that does a lot of winning at Open show level, the temptation to try the Championship show becomes very strong. At the back of one's mind is the hope, the dream, of achieving the ultimate acclaim and making up a Champion. But, Champion or not, at the end of the day we are still taking the same dog home. Classes are very often the same at the Open shows but incorporate the dog and the bitch, for example the class called Novice Dog or Bitch.

BREED CLUB OPEN SHOWS attract far larger entries than the ordinary Open show. They are open to all, not just club members, and they usually have more classes, including colour classes and stake classes and those for pet trims.

EXEMPTION SHOWS are usually held in conjunction with a village fete or are run in aid of charity. One meets a wide range of dog fanciers at Exemption shows, from the pet owner with his cross-breed rascal, which has probably never had a bath in its life, let alone a good brushing, to the more professional breeder/exhibitor who wishes to use the local shows to gain experience for a youngster destined for the show ring at a higher level. There are some dog-

showing enthusiasts who love Exemption shows and they go around from one to the next. I must add that, very often, the best of prizes are on offer at the Exemption show. Once, I even won a trialing ribbon on which was embossed the word Champion. This is totally incorrect. Under Kennel Club rules no dog is entitled to carry the title of Champion unless it has won that title at Championship shows.

SANCTION AND LIMITED SHOWS are rare these days and are usually restricted to members of a club.

MATCHES are usually run by a local training club and they are friendly and good fun for novice dog and owner. Use Matches to gain experience and meet other dog enthusiasts. Dogs are judged one against one in a knock-out competition. It is usual to have a Best Puppy and a Best of Match.

ENTERING SHOWS
Exemption shows are the only shows that one can enter on the day. The usual procedure is to obtain a schedule for the show, fill it in and send it to the secretary of the show before the date of closing which is normally about six weeks before the show. All shows are advertised in the weekly dog press.

At Championship shows the judges have to be experienced and need to be passed by the Kennel Club to award CCs. Some Open show societies are careful about the judges they choose for a breed, others are not. Good handling does contribute to how much a dog can win, as does presentation. A beautifully turned out and handled Standard Poodle will almost always beat a better dog that does not look so good and is untrained.

Two dogs with the same qualities will be classed in order of merit by the handling and presentation. Well, would you prefer Miss World in rags or riches? If you cannot bear not to win then please do not show dogs. It can be soul-destroying at the best of times. I can only say, if your dog is good enough, is turned out to perfection, and you are an expert handler with the patience of a saint, you may get there in the end!

SHOWS IN THE USA

As is the case in the UK, Americans have different types of shows which they can enter. However, showing or exhibiting in America is very different because mainly it is done by professional handlers. Dogs and handlers travel thousands of miles across states to compete at Championship level.

ALL BREED CHAMPIONSHIP

SHOWS are as popular in America as they are in Britain, although entries are smaller. Points are on offer at these Championship shows which count towards the title of Champion. Some of these shows are run with the support of a breed club.

SPECIALTY SHOWS attract larger entries. Many states hold these shows, where Sweepstakes classes are scheduled for the younger dogs, having a separate judge and giving the dogs an extra chance to win.

MATCHES are small shows and exclude Champions. They are normally held by a specialised club or an all-breed club which does not offer Championship points.

There are many more Championship shows in the USA than in the UK. Entries however, are fewer in number except at some of the notable Specialty Shows, which are immensely popular. At some of the All Breed Shows where 'Supported Entries', with the backing of special prizes from a breed club or the judge (the latter being a practice that is rarely seen in the UK), a higher entry is often achieved. The Matches are

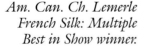

Am. Can. Ch. Lemerle French Silk: Multiple Best in Show winner.

Photo: Wayne Cott.

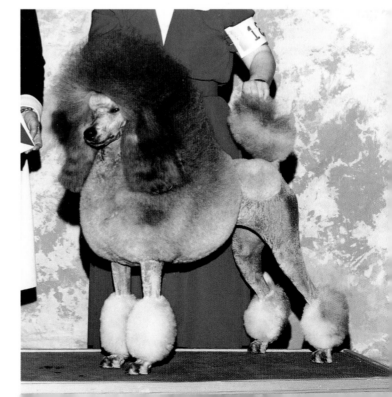

probably on about the same level as the Exemption Show in the UK and not to be equated with the club and inter-club Matches we see in the UK where one dog is judged against another in a knockout fashion.

CHAMPION QUALIFICATIONS
UK: For a dog to gain the Coveted Title of Champion it must win a total of three Challenge Certificates (CCs) from three different judges at Championship shows. The third CC must be won after the dog has reached the age of twelve months. A Res. CC is given to the runner-up in each sex but this does not count towards a title. In Britain there is no Champion class, so in order to win a CC a dog must beat all Champions present. A young dog can win a Junior Warrant by winning twenty-five points between the age of twelve and eighteen months. This is not a title. Points can be won at Open and Championship shows.

USA: A total of fifteen points is required before a dog can carry the title of Champion, of which two blocks are Majors awarded by different judges. A Major is three, four or five points. Five points are the maximum allotted. Points are dependent on the number of dogs competing and are reviewed on a yearly basis. If the number of bitches exceeds that of dogs the points awarded are regulated accordingly. Champions do not compete for points; they are entered in the Best of Breed Class. The Winners of the Regular Classes go forward to meet the Champions to compete for Best of Sex. Extra points are awarded to a dog when he beats a Champion for Best of Sex.

EIRE: The Irish Kennel Club governs dog shows in Eire; Northern Ireland is governed by the English Kennel Club. The Irish Champion is won on a points system. Points awarded are dependent upon the number of exhibits at a particular show. To become a Champion, Green Stars to the total of forty points must be won, of which four must be of five points or more, or two wins of ten points obtainable at special shows. Some special shows carry a guaranteed Major irrespective of the number of dogs shown. The dog and bitch awards do not always carry the same amount of points but the Best of Breed winner receives the same points as the opposite sex winner where the opposite sex had the highest number of exhibits. Dogs must be registered with the Irish KC to show in Southern Ireland.

SCANDINAVIAN COUNTRIES: Ken Bullock, a renowned Poodle man, who judges all over the world, kindly informed me that there are probably hundreds of countries which come under FCI rules – practically every country, in fact, that does not speak English, although Ireland and, now, Australia, are members of the FCI. A dog can start competing for certificates from the age of nine months. The certificate is awarded to a Winners Class, for which the dog has to qualify on the day. This class is not open to Champions. In Winners Class the judge can hand out several – or no – awards of Champion quality. If the winning dog gets this award, it is also awarded a certificate. To become a Champion in Sweden a Standard Poodle has to win three certificates under at least two different judges, and at least one of the certificates must be won after the age of 24 months. All dogs, including Champions and

Veterans go on to the Best of Sex competition. At International shows, the CACIB (International Certificate) is awarded in this class.

To become an International Champion, a Standard Poodle must win four CACIBs under at least three different judges, with at least one year between the first and the last CACIB, and in at least three countries, one of which has to be the owner's home country or the breed's country of origin. For Standard Poodles, two CACIBs are awarded in each sex – one for blacks, browns and whites, and one for silvers and apricots. The dog can start competing for CACIB at the age of 15 months. Before becoming an International Champion, the dog has to be a National Champion. There are only minor differences in Denmark and Finland.

NUCH Sharp Dressed Isadora, based in Norway.

TRAINING THE SHOW DOG

So, now that you know a little about showing, it is time to train that dog. All puppies are full of energy, or they should be. They sleep a lot and they play a lot. Standard Poodles, being possessed of a devilish spirit for the ridiculous, can upturn you when least expected. Although you train your puppy to perfection, do not be too surprised if, on his first or second appearance in the show ring, he acts the proper clown. If you feel like taking the puppy out of the ring and beating it for showing you up, please do not show a Standard Poodle. Or better still, please do not own one. If you can laugh at your dog's clownish, eye-catching antics, then you are half-way to winning.

With puppies it is better to train a little each day for a week or so, then twice, or even once a week is enough for Standard Poodles. They are very intelligent and can become bored. A disinterested dog does not make a good show dog. However, most Standard Poodles love to show off and they thoroughly enjoy their day at a show. Having said that, puppies do get tired very quickly and a day at a show for a puppy of six months is extremely exhausting. Older dogs need a day of rest to recover from a show, a puppy will need more, especially if you have had to travel quite a distance in order to get to the show.

THE CORRECT STANCE

Assuming you have done some homework, visited local shows to watch the proceedings, looked at photographs of great dogs in the dog papers and in good books, and attended show ring training classes to see how it is all done and to socialise the pup, you will have some idea of the correct stance for

SHOW TRAINING
Photos: Steph Holbrook.

THE SHOW POSE

1. *Walk your Standard Poodle into the stand.*

2. *Place the front leg under the shoulder.*

3. *Place the hindleg so that it stands beneath the tip of the tail.*

4. *Standing behind to check the dog is standing correctly.*

5. *Checking the topline.*

6. Stacked for the show ring – a technique commonly used in the UK and the USA.

7. Holding the dog closer to the neck – also frequently seen in the show ring.

showing off the virtues of your lovely Poodle. Some handlers free-stand their dogs. Others 'top and tail' them, holding the head up under the chin and holding up the tip of the tail. I have to say it does not matter which way you choose; both are considered correct. It really depends on the dog you are handling. Some dogs hate being fussed and will show their hearts out unaided. Other dogs like more contact and prefer to be held close. Dogs can be trained to stand both ways but if your dog is happier in one particular way, go with it.

Your puppy will have become acquainted with being groomed and clipped on the table. Now, after brushing him, tell him to stand. Place a finger of one hand under his chin, and the other hand gently underneath his tummy, being careful not to push his back upwards. Progress to making sure that his front legs are beneath his shoulders and that his back legs are placed with the toes beneath the base of his tail. Young

puppies are not usually balanced, or grown enough to stand square, so do not be over-fussy about stance to begin with. Hopefully, if your dog's tail is correctly set on, he will carry this high naturally – high, but away from the body, as required in the Breed Standard. If the pup needs some encouragement with its tail then gently coax this up until it stands at ten-to-two. Poodles should never have their tails over their backs.

Once you have attained the desired result of getting your Standard Poodle to show-stand on the table, progress to the floor, repeating the exercise. If your dog has the correct conformation he can easily be trained to walk into the stand without too much interference from you. Have the dog at your left side, take a few steps, come to a halt, warning the dog you are going to stop by first using his name, then give the command Stand. You hold the lead up as you come to a halt, putting slight tension on the neck.

ABOVE: *Moving your dog for the judge to assess overall conformation.*

CENTRE: *Moving away from the judge.*

RIGHT: *Moving towards the judge.*

WALKING AND TROTTING

Next you must teach the dog to walk and trot beside you on a loose lead. Keep the dog on your left, with the loose lead in your left hand. Trot, or, in the case of young puppies, walk. It is not so much that you need to do this quickly, but that you must use big strides in order to encourage the dog to move freely forward. If you have a good relationship with your dog, he will move close to you quite naturally. If he is out of control, either you have not read the previous chapters and taken note, or your puppy is feeling rather exuberant. In the latter case let him have a run round to expel some energy before you start training.

Be sure to take a nice straight line when you move. Aim at something solid and walk towards it, encouraging your Poodle to walk beside you with the aid of your voice. If your pup pulls rather too enthusiastically, check it back with a quick jerk of the lead. If the pup drags behind he is either tired or worried. Use lots of encouragement, or pack up for the day.

Having reached your destination, turn in a reasonable left-hand U to come back to where you started. This is called a show turn; the dog is between you and the judge at all times. This turn is executed so that the judge can watch and assess the dog without your legs obscuring his vision.

Now try a triangle. Go away to the right-hand corner of your imaginary ring, with the dog on left side. Move straight across the top of the ring, then come back from the left, stopping about one metre in front of where you started – where stands your imaginary judge. We do not want to knock the judge over, do we?

It is also advisable to train on a circle, as the judge will run the class round the ring, all together, to settle the exhibits and to take a quick assessment before looking at the dogs individually. With training it is always a good idea to run and walk on both diagonals. In other words, if you implement a left-hand circle twice, do the same on the right. This will ensure balance of muscles and add interest for the dog.

A properly trained dog hardly needs a lead. There is nothing worse than trying to assess a lovely dog who constantly turns somersaults or whose owner strings it up hangman fashion. Remember basic puppy training. If you pull your dog on a tight lead, it will pull you back. Most judges are convinced that those handlers that hang their dogs, who string their necks up, are trying to disguise a bad front.

STANDING FOR ASSESSMENT
Now your Standard Poodle must learn to stand still while the judge assesses him, 'goes over' him. The judge will look into the dog's face to see its eyes and shape of the head, check the teeth for correctness, feel the leathers for quality, width and length, and feel the shoulder placement, ribcage, back and quarters.

Because Standard Poodles are friendly it is relatively easy to train them to stand still for a few minutes while the judge feels over them. Sometimes, in early puppy training, your Poodle will want to jump up at the judge and lick their face – or, in the case of my Samantha, pinch the judge's rosette! This enthusiasm must be deterred through gentle remonstration – you do not want to put your puppy off for ever. First, get your puppy to stand while you go over it, kindly but firmly. When the pup is happy with this, get an experienced friend to go over him; then an experienced stranger. I say experienced, because if a person does not understand ring procedure you are wasting your time. Do not spend too much time with this assessment. Judges take only a minute or two to evaluate a dog.

STARTING SHOWING
You have decided to take the plunge! Then my advice is to attend your local show ring training classes. Most pet shops or the local newspaper can give you the address of your nearest society that runs show training classes. These classes are great confidence-boosters for the dog and for the novice handler. They are excellent for socialising, less strenuous on a puppy than obedience classes and often more friendly. Puppies are welcome as soon as their vaccinations are complete.

Allow your puppy to play with other puppies at ring training. Also it is a good idea to let people give your pup a tidbit in order to make friends. Remember, early socialisation is the key to success in gaining a happy, secure and confident temperament. Do not be strict or apply compulsion at early puppy training classes. Many show ring training classes run monthly matches which simulate small shows. These are good practice for dog and owner. Soon you will be itching to try a few Exemption shows, then that Open show. Next you will want to progress to Championship level. Good luck!

JUDGING

I do not pretend to know all there is to know about judging dogs. My opinion is that we never stop learning. I am grateful to my mentors for passing on valuable knowledge, but especially to Mavis of the Beguinette Standard Poodles for taking the time to sit on a bench with me at a show, when I was just eighteen years old, to answer my question: "What did the judge mean in her show report when she said my bitch was well angulated?" Mavis drew me a diagram and explained to me about lay-back of shoulder etc. I was so fascinated that the very next day I purchased my first book on anatomy.

What does still shock me is that there are judges who step into the ring who have no knowledge of anatomy at all. I appreciate that all the reading in the world will not give a person that quality of possessing a good eye. But, if you can recognise a good dog from instinctive talent, why not try to understand the virtues placed before you. Inexperienced judges try to balance one fault against another. I do not believe that is the way forward.

The accepted concept of a dog show is to find the best dogs, placing them in order of merit. The idea is that the constant winners will be bred from to further the progress of the breed. This is the one and only consideration towards which the judge must aim. Different judges will have their preferences and there is nothing wrong with that. However, good temperament must be the greatest virtue of any Standard Poodle.

JUDGING IS AN ART

Without artistic flair, or a natural, instinctive sense, it is not possible to recognise and assess that which cannot be touched – type, quality, balance, expression and temperament. Natural intuition, a good eye for a dog, is an essential quality in a good judge. Sad to say not all judges possess such artistic intellect. No amount of study can supply this skill. However, we do have many excellent judges around the world in the show ring today. I hope I can inspire aspiring judges to seek a deeper understanding of the Standard Poodle. We all make mistakes, and I do not suppose the perfect judge is any more possible to attain than the perfect dog. If we try to comprehend, and to strive for perfection, we may develop the eye to recognise a masterpiece, or just appreciate the virtues a dog possesses to pass on to prosperity.

JUDGING IS A SCIENCE

It is easy to identify those judges who do not have a sound knowledge of anatomy. How dare they step into the ring? They feel over a dog because they have watched other judges do so. Really, they have no idea about the lay-back of shoulder (scapula), the upper arm angle (humerus), and the depth and spring of rib (sternum and sternal ribs), because they do not have sufficient knowledge to understand angulation and its effect. To find a dog with a crooked tooth, or a long back, or a gay tail is relatively simple – well, it is to some – but all dogs have faults and to judge one fault against another is naive and unproductive. Far better for the breed is the judge that looks for positive virtues – something which is worth handing down. A Standard Poodle may have a wonderful coat and be prepared to a standard of perfection that will dazzle the eye and draw attention, a dog may be a real flashy show-off, but if it has a coarse

100

head with big round eyes and loose rolls of skin round its neck, or if it has a substandard frame, narrow ribs and weak quarters, it will be of no use in furthering the breed's progress. To my mind it is essential to study anatomy before breeding, let alone judging.

WAYS TO LEARN

All judges must be prepared to study the Kennel Clubs' Standards for the breed. These do vary slightly in different parts of the world but the basic structure is the same. We go through these and try to attain a sensible balance. All judges must understand and judge by the Standard of the breed to the best of their ability. The judge's word is final. If you love Standard Poodles enough to want to judge, read the Breed Standard, go through it, together with experienced judges of the breed, on several different specimens. Recognise faults but consider, more essentially, the virtues a dog has, with a view to them being handed on to prosperity. Read about other breeds and make comparisons; this will open your eyes to the qualities of the different breeds, and prevent a closed attitude of mind.

MUSCLE QUALITY

It is essential to study bone structure and to be aware of any deviation from that which is essentially correct. However, it is also vitally important to have some understanding of muscle formation. Delving into anatomic names is not really necessary for the moment. All we really need to recognise is what to expect, in the way of performance, from the feel of muscle quality.

Say we have a dog whose construction is essentially correct. This is a dog whose owner is a whiz at presentation and the dog looks perfect. But this is a dog

which lives in a cage or small kennel to protect its coat, whose daily exercise is restricted to a controlled pen. This dog will not develop the hard flesh and strong elastic-band muscles to sustain powerful movement. Some breeders produce excellent dogs that cannot move with any effective quality. Exercise these good dogs and see what a tremendous difference it makes to their movement. It is not only bad training and bad construction that produces bad movers, it is also the lack of effective muscle.

Building heavy muscle is not a substitute for an inferior skeleton. However, get the balance right and we have a fine dog of quality that can move freely in poetic lines. Given a good handler, a Standard Poodle, correctly constructed, with good-quality muscle power to keep that structure from falling apart on the move, is a joy to behold.

Some dogs will build excess muscle on a weak joint such as the ball and socket hip joint. Muscle can be affected when there is a weak or damaged stifle joint, or over-angulation. The dog will often, such is nature's way, compensate for poor bone by building heavy muscle to support the fragile frame or structure. A good way of identifying underlining problems is to find a dog whose muscle formation is unbalanced. In other words, if the dog has generally poor muscle power, and yet, on the hips, we feel that it is plump and overloaded, this is an indication of trouble. It is not the judge's job to decide why a dog has such problems. If the dog cannot move, walk, trot and run with substance and be effective in a light, free and easy manner, then it must be penalised.

LEARNING RING PROCEDURE

Obviously any person taking up judging

has been showing dogs for at least ten years, has bred a Champion or two and is dedicated to their particular breed. They will know the general procedure of standing in the middle of the ring, of being properly dressed, of going over, and of assessing the movement of the dogs placed before them. I do advise prospective judges to attend ring training classes and to ask to take the class. Most training classes have an experienced

judge or two as trainers. Invaluable knowledge can be gained from these judges and by assimilating ring procedure. This will give the new judge experience and confidence. At these classes it is not essential to have a sound understanding of every breed. But, please, do try to have a sound comprehension of a breed before you accept a judging appointment.

7 *THE VERSATILE STANDARD POODLE*

Standard Poodles are about a lot more than just show dogs. They make wonderful companions – you are never alone with a Standard Poodle! Yet there is more. Because the Poodle has a coat which can be groomed to make it look smart, it is taken advantage of in a way that gives people the impression that the Poodle is nothing more than a cream puff. It is most unfortunate that among Standard Poodle owners who profess to adore the breed, we have those who use these dogs to draw attention to themselves. They use dye to colour white poodles pink, or lilac, or even green. What an undignified way to take advantage of a dog who is capable of performing just about any feat we ask of it. Here are a few tasks in which the Standard Poodle excels, gaining them the acclaim they deserve.

WORKING
The original Poodle was a working, hunting, herding, scenting, retrieving, tracking dog of such sensitivity and gentleness that it surpassed all other breeds in its activities. Perhaps its downfall, or drawback, was its coat,

which needed considerable attention compared to the short-haired working dogs, or even the Spaniel or Setter. For many years the Standard Poodle has been noted for its outstanding nature, but today this accomplished breed still retains its eminent ability to work – given the opportunity. In many parts of the world the Standard Poodle works in tests; predominantly Canada, USA, Australia and some of the Scandinavian countries seem to take an interest in retaining the inherent ability of this versatile breed.

FIELD EVENTS
On October 22nd 1995, the first-ever West Coast all-Poodle Field Training event took place, near Lodi, California. Twelve Standard Poodle owners gathered together to assess their dogs' ability to work as retrievers, fetching bumpers, a dead bird and a duck wing from water. Some owners were concerned that their Poodles had forgotten all about their ancestral instinct to enter water. How I often wish I could breed out that instinct in my Poodles! Living, as I do, adjoining a nature reserve, where my Standard

HR. Ch. Bibelot's Silver Power Play CDX: The Standard Poodle can still be trained to perform the tasks it was originally bred for.

Photo: Shirley Nelson.

Poodles are walked daily, it is all I can do to keep them from jumping into the lagoons before I can shout NO! Often Goldie has fetched a duck (or some rare species of visiting bird) for my approval. Luckily she does not hurt the objecting bird and it is freed to go on its way. As to retrieving a dead duck's wing? I am sure my lot would eat it!

Back to the serious historical event at Lodi. Very few of the twelve Standard Poodles taking part had done any previous field work, although most were trained in basic retrieve. Over half the dogs present accomplished the goal of retrieving from water by the end of the day. Which says a lot for the Standard Poodle's ability to respond to sensible requests. The next step is to persuade the AKC to permit Poodles to compete for Hunting Titles.

HUNTING POODLES

Today the Standard Poodle still carries its original hunting genes. With no training at all those instincts give the Standard Poodle the ability to locate game, something my dogs do on a daily basis during their morning walk. Trained, the Standard Poodle is as indispensable to a bird hunter as any working bird dog.

Hunt tests are probably more demanding than the real thing. Dogs must have the suitable temperament to withstand gun noise, they are required to swim through decoys and reeds, to stay with you in duck blinds, and to crash through heavy thickets and undergrowth, up and down gullies and climb in and out of boats. The senses of sight, sound, smell, and touch (mouth) are used as the dog seeks his retrieve of wounded or dead birds. Hand and whistle commands are given to the more advanced dogs. The Hunt Tests are to encourage owners to develop their dogs' natural skills. In North America and Canada the dog is tested against a Standard; the dogs do not compete against each other.

At the time of writing the AKC does not allow Standard Poodles to compete in their Hunt Tests because it does not recognise the Poodle as a 'retrieving' breed. Other clubs award hunting titles to Poodles because they are included within their gundog group.

The Working Certificate, WC or WCX (Working Certificate Excellent), is awarded to qualifying Standard Poodles in North America. For anybody interested in the training of a Standard Poodle in hunting and working I suggest you read a good book on the subject and then join a club involved in these activities.

In New Mexico, on the historic day of October 22nd 1995, Eileen Jaskowski made history with her eighteen-month-old Standard Poodle, Pie, who was bred by Susan Fraser. Pie appeared at an American Kennel Club Hunt Test to demonstrate the test conditions for the participating dogs. He ran in both Junior Hunter and Senior Hunter tests with outstanding success. In fact, Eileen says that Pie was the only dog of the day to go directly into the blind retrieve – this refers to a retrieve of a bird that the dog never saw thrown – without having to be stopped and redirected by the handler. Pie has now completed his Utility title. The aim now is to get the AKC to allow Poodles their right to compete for Hunting Test Titles.

GAINING A WORKING CERTIFICATE
These are the performance requirements for a PCA Working Certificate, a WC or a Working Certificate Excellent.
1) Retrieval of two single birds at approximately 50 yards on land for WC and a double bird mark at approximately 75 yards on land with an honour, for WCX.
2) Retrieval of two single birds from water to prove willingness to re-enter

water for WC and a double bird mark from water for WCX.
3) The dog may be held on a line, as steadiness is not required for WC; the dog must be steady on the line for WCX.
4) The dog must not show fear of guns.
5) These requirements may be met in several ways:
a. completing the land and water retrieves in an approved field test;
b. completing a WC Test or WCX Test held by an approved Retriever Club;
c. completing a hunt test of equal or greater difficulty held by an approved Hunt Club. (The Poodle Club of America).

WORKING TRIALS IN CANADA
Canadian Kennel Club retriever (and Irish Water Spaniel) WC/I/X rules were first adopted in 1981 for implementation in 1992. The first test was in Winnipeg May 1982, then in Ontario in June 1982. Standard Poodles were permitted to run in these tests thanks to a letter of request from Jacqueline Harbour (Tudorose), formerly from Cambridge, England. The first WC awarded to a Poodle was on June 29th 1986. Standard Poodles were allowed to participate in CKC retriever Hunt Tests from their commencement in April 1996. The inspiration to compete in these tests is credited to AKC all-breed judge and Poodle breeder Charles Le Boutillier and his illustrated lectures.

STANDARD POODLES IN OBEDIENCE
Standard Poodles have become a familiar sight in the Obedience ring at all levels in many countries of the world. Shows are held under Kennel Club rules, and Clubs, which can be found in most areas, are registered with the Kennel Club. Most

Marie Patchell with Namika Micaela (Brillo) at the Poodle Training Club Obedience Show.

Photos: Bob Ratcliffe.

public libraries keep records of established clubs and where they hold their classes. Very often a novice dog owner will start early training by participating in the Kennel Clubs Citizen Award Scheme designed to encourage dog owners to train their dogs to be a credit in society. Many owners then decide to take training a step further and join the regular Obedience classes.

Obedience tests or shows cater for all levels from the Pre-Beginner, Novice, Class A and Class B to the top of the league Class C. Dogs win their way through these classes with the tests becoming progressively more difficult. Where Challenge Certificates are on offer, three of these must be won for the dog to hold the title of Champion.

Over the years Standard Poodles have excelled in Obedience Tests, though it is true to say few Standard Poodle owners take this form of activity with serious intent. As a breed they learn easily and are quick on their feet considering their size. It is essential to allow a Standard Poodle to grow to full maturity before starting any serious training or competing in Obedience. Bone damage can, and has, resulted from too much stress on joints, as well as the early onset of arthritis. A young working dog is under tremendous strain.

Standard Poodles love learning new things, but be warned, they easily get bored with repetition which they find unnecessary. One of my Standards, Jane, decided to teach me a lesson one day in an Obedience test. I threw the dumbbell and she went to fetch it as usual. Then she picked it up with a devil of mischief glinting in her eyes, and promptly jumped on a spare seat at the ringside, sitting upright beside a lady spectator, dumbbell still in mouth. Just as Jane predicted, everybody watching collapsed into fits of laughter. Once Jane had made her point – shown me that I was getting far too serious in my application – Jane returned to me to complete her retrieve,

Von Silbertal Narayan UD: Multiple highest score in Obedience Trial winner, Obedience Dog of the Year, Poodle Cub of Victoria, Australia, 1995 and 1996, member of Pal Superdog Obedience, Agility and Flyball team. Bred by E. Zimmerman, trained by Linda Johnson.

Aust. Ch. Chezvistra Undacova Girl UD, TD, AD, ET: Successful in Obedience, Agility, Tracking and Conformation, as well as passing an Endurance Test. Bred by J.A. & J. Viera, trained by Jenni Staniforth.

as though she had not a care in the world.

Standard Poodles are fun dogs and I think it is for that reason their owners tend to be fun people. Obedience Tests and the repetition of training very often find the Poodle and owner longing for a more interesting and entertaining pursuit, such as some of the activities that follow.

AGILITY

Many affiliated Obedience clubs now hold Agility classes and shows under Kennel Club rules. Dogs exceeding 18 calendar months can participate in Competition. The Competition does vary for the size and ability of the dog. Classes run through from Elementary, Starters, Intermediate and Seniors to Advance and Open. Courses include obstacles such as hurdles, a rising spread jump, a brush fence, a hoop or tyre, a table, a long jump, a water jump, the wishing well or lychgate, the collapsible tunnel, the pipe tunnel, weaving poles, the pause box, a ramp, a see-saw, a dog-walk and cross-over.

Agility is great fun for handler and dog. It is no wonder it is becoming an increasingly popular pastime among dog owners throughout many different parts of the world. Many people find Agility more interesting than Obedience work and it is probably far more suited to the Standard Poodle's sense of fun. It is, however, essential for Agility dogs to be taught the rudiments of basic Obedience.

LEFT: *Aust. Ch. Neiger Circus Rose CDX: Multiple highest score in Obedience Trial winner, highest scoring Poodle at Melbourne Royal Show 1996, member of Pal Superdog Obedience, Agility and Flyball team, multiple Best of Breed winner in the conformation ring. Bred by N. & G. Robertson, trained by Linda Johnson.*

And it goes without saying – dog and handler have to be blessed with stamina and be fit and healthy.

FLYBALL
Flyball is closely associated with Agility. This is a great spectator sport which includes a team knockout competition. The idea is that the dog runs the course of hurdles, reaches a box and triggers it to dispatch a ball, which it then carries in its mouth while promptly returning to its handler. Addresses for Flyball, Agility and Obedience clubs can usually be found at the local library. Failing that if you are interested in any aspect of dog

sports then do visit a local dog show – advertised in the local papers or the dog press – and enquire among competitors for a satisfactory dog club.

GUIDE DOGS FOR THE BLIND

Lesley Kelly made history in Britain when she agreed to take on a Standard Poodle as a guide dog. After she had failed to cope with two other guide dogs, a Labrador and a Golden Retriever, along came Valda. Because of the arthritis Lesley suffers along with her blindness, it was necessary for her to have a gentle dog that was easily controllable. Valda, the Standard Poodle, has proved to be perfect. She has given Lesley the confidence to walk to the shops and the bus stop. Remarkably, together they take the train to London, sometimes as often as twice a week, from their home in Coventry.

Valda causes a sensation wherever she goes. As well as being unique as the first Standard Poodle Guide Dog in Britain, she attracts attention with her dignified presence. She has proved to Lesley that a Standard Poodle makes a perfect guide for the blind. Intelligent enough to steer Lesley around obstacles and through traffic, Valda has made life for Lesley not only far less difficult, but also a lot happier as it is now full and productive.

Lesley admits to having been very sceptical on her first introduction to Valda. "I put my hands on the black blob that I could just visualise, and I got the shock of my life. As soon as I felt Valda's coat I knew she was a Poodle and misgivings filled my senses," she says. Lesley had never met a Standard Poodle before being introduced to Valda. But they were soon to make friends. Valda loved a fuss being made of her. She had been puppy-walked – that is raised, and

Guide dog Valda with her owner Lesley Kelly.
Photo: Chris Dawson.

socialised from a tiny puppy of about seven weeks old to an age where she was mentally and physically capable of beginning her training – first by a school teacher who took her to school to mix with the children as well as getting her accustomed to noise, and then by a child-minder. She had therefore developed the characteristic friendly temperament of the Standard Poodle. She nudged Lesley for attention, sat close to her beside her chair and rested her head in Lesley's lap. Both Valda and Lesley seemed content with each other. At this early stage it was decided that Valda's training would continue to suit Lesley's requirements.

Emma with Janavons Beryl The Peril: The good-natured Standard Poodle excels as a therapy dog,
Photo: Peterborough Evening Telegraph.

Lorraine aged six, loving every second of her visit from Janavons Beryl The Peril and Janavons Denim.
Photo: Peterborough Evening Telegraph.

They were both installed in the training centre at Leamington for training to be completed together, which was for a period of about six weeks.

Lesley very soon came to admit that her misgivings were misplaced. Valda guided her around obstacles with the greatest of ease. "She was gentle, confident and moved at precisely the right pace for me. We were soon firm friends."

Because of the total success of Valda as a guide dog, other Standard Poodles are sure to follow. However, the major difficulty is that there is the extra expense of having a Poodle trimmed at the Poodle Parlour every six weeks, and the blind person has to learn to groom the Poodle coat daily to prevent it from forming into mats and tangles. Lesley says she has come to cope with this fairly well but it is far easier to cope with the coat when it has just been bathed and trimmed. But it is all worthwhile, according to Lesley, who is becoming increasingly reliant on her stately, if somewhat unconventional companion.

I was privileged to meet Valda and

Lesley. They make an impressive and stirring team together. Lesley now has her freedom and independence and she feels confidently secure with Valda at her side. "My Standard Poodle Guide Dog is brilliant!" she says.

THERAPY DOGS
Pets as Therapy Dogs, Pat-Dogs as they are called in the UK, are dogs which are registered with the Pro-Dogs organisation to establish good relationships in special circumstances. They have to pass a stringent temperament test before they are considered suitable to take on such a responsible and significant task as visiting nursing homes, residential homes, hospices and special schools, and other establishments that feel that the bond between man and dog will enhance the human's quality of life. Pat-Dogs have proved to be wonderful healers and confidence boosters. They most certainly do have a substantial therapeutic effect on the sick, the elderly and the mentally and physically disabled.

I know my Standard Poodles are even-tempered, but when I was first asked to visit a school of mentally handicapped children, I must admit to having been slightly apprehensive. Neither the dogs or I had had any experience with these special children. The headmistress of Orchard Court School at that time, Yvonne Barker, was convinced, after reading about therapy dogs, that her pupils would benefit from getting to know about dogs. I took two of my registered therapy dogs, Rainbow and Denim, along for them to make friends with the children. It only took a few minutes for me to realise these dogs were far better adjusted mentally to coping with this unusual situation than I had

given them credit for.

The disabilities of some children, especially autistic children, force them to live in a world of their own. It was hoped, in time, that a bond would be cemented between the dogs and the children. In fact, a friendship sprang up with immediate impact. The class of 13 to 15 year-olds were soon smiling from ear to ear when Rainbow and Denim nudged them for attention. We had introduced the dogs during the tea break and it was only moments before Denim and Rainbow were sharing biscuits with the laughing children. Even an autistic boy who liked to keep to his own corner found himself interested in these strange furry dogs.

Having established a good relationship with the older children, the dogs were then introduced to a class of about twelve five to seven-year-olds. Some of these children had never had any contact with a dog at all. They were very frightened. But the Standard Poodle who is socially trained is very clever at winning friends. With a gentleness one has to see to believe, Denim approached an almost hysterically nervous child by crawling along the floor on his belly. At first this little girl screamed in horror, but soon she became curious about this wriggling ball of fluff and gingerly, with encouragement from me, reached out to feel it. This frightened youngster, named Emma, developed a particular and special bond with the dogs and changed from being cringing and apprehensive into a happy and confident little girl. The active therapy achieved its purpose.

THE LIFESAVER
Jeanne Eve's Standard Poodle, Dana, had always been Jeanne's prized and treasured pet, but even Jeanne was

touched to the heart when Dana was responsible for saving her brother Peter's life. At a family gathering, with everybody sharing a drink and catching up on gossip, Dana suddenly got up from her place on the floor at Jeanne's side, crossed the room and sat directly before Peter, staring into his eyes.

Presently, after being ignored, Dana returned to Jeanne to paw her. Having gained Jeanne's attention, Dana immediately returned to her sitting place in front of Peter, who was sitting slightly away from the crowd in a chair overlooking the garden. Then Dana dropped her head to her chest and began to whine. Now alerted, Jeanne pointed out this strange behaviour to Peter's daughter Bianca. After taking one look at her father, Bianca called for an ambulance. Peter was falling into a diabetic coma.

Dana had somehow sensed that Peter was in trouble several minutes before even he was aware of anything abnormal. Had Dana not alerted Jeanne and Bianca when she did, the chat and occupation may well have proceeded without anybody being aware of the dangerous condition Peter was succumbing to. Jeanne and Bianca, and Peter himself, are convinced Dana saved a life.

SLED DOGS IN ALASKA.
In the depths of some of the meanest country, where the nights are so frozen in winter that a slight breeze hits your face like a steel blade, lives the man they call John 'Standard Poodle Man' Suter and his team of triumphant dogs. The zoologist Desmond Morris once described the Poodle as 'a triumph of human frivolity'. To John Suter he is a creature of immense value. "They are a dog of great intelligence and versatility," he says.

In 1976 John Suter launched a team of Standard Poodles into the highly competitive world of sled racing. Other competitors considered John's Poodles to be nothing more than a joke – especially as this first short race turned out a total disaster when John's dogs headed straight for the local park. Undaunted, John's firm character and true belief in his Standard Poodles' qualities convinced him that, having hit the bottom, there was only one way to go – up!

Fifteen years, six generations of dogs and with more than 180 races covering 20,000 miles later, John reached his goal. John's Standard Poodles have pulled him across mountain ranges, frozen seas, up the canyons and over passes of the Iditaroil trail, through blizzards, howling gales and weather so cold it is impossible to believe. John's dogs are among the toughest in the world. They have competed what is considered to be the Last Great Race on Earth, covering 1,100 miles of snow and ice between Anchorage and Nome, Alaska. Twice John's Standard Poodles have won the 'belt buckle' for finishing, once in 14 days, once in 16 days.

Originally John had considered the Standard Poodle to be nothing more than a rich, pampered pet which belonged on a velvet chaise longue, certainly not on the icy waters of Alaska. John had his eyes opened to the amazing talents and ability of the Poodle when he was asked by his father-in-law to look after his pampered, pom-pom-adorned

FACING PAGE: John Suter has now raced more than 20,000 miles with his Standard Poodles.

SLED RACING
Photos: Gerald Davis.

The Standard Poodle shows tremendous enthusiasm for the work, despite the harsh conditions.

The Poodles are not clipped, and they wear coats at the rest stops.

Training depends on encouragement and firm control.

pet Fluette. He took Fluette out for a drive on his Sno-Cat, and was astounded when the Poodle leapt from the Sno-Cat to race alongside in the snow, yelping with sheer excitement. So impressed was he that John decided to look into what made a Poodle. He was intrigued by its ancestry of being a retrieving and water-working dog and decided to try them out on one of the toughest assignments a dog could endure. He now firmly believes that because the Poodle has a coat which can be 'fancied up' they have long had a bad rap.

The Husky is the native dog of the wild Chuguah Mountains and the Northern Parks and is essential to everyday life. Every house, hut or igloo has a couple of dogs. The dogs are the lifeline in this mass of white, silent land. John says that Poodles, when reared alongside the Huskies, grow to think like them. "My training approach puts the psychological well-being of the team high on the priority list. Harsh discipline is never used, but happy-go-lucky

encouragement and firm control are," he says. The Poodles only differ in their ability to withstand extreme cold. To overcome this problem John sprays the Standard Poodles with sealant spray. And he puts coats on them to help retain body heat at the rest stops. Of course, John's Poodles are not bathed and clipped or groomed as the pet and show dog we are accustomed to seeing. They would never withstand the ferocious weather as pampered pets. So significant are John's Standard Poodles, they are now becoming known as the canine equivalent of the SAS.

The Standard Poodles have proved through their great ability, strength of character, and enthusiasm to do a job, and their tremendous loyalty that they are certainly no joke. John Suter holds the award of 'belt buckle' to prove it. I am indebted to the top journalist Rod Tyler for helping me track down John Suter.

115

8 *BREEDING STANDARD POODLES*

When you have a good bitch which has been doing a lot of winning in the show ring, you may consider breeding your first litter of puppies, However, breeding from a family pet needs serious thought, no matter how nice she is. If she is your only Standard Poodle and something goes wrong and you lose her, the pain you will suffer will be considerable. I once lost a three-year-old bitch having her first litter. She needed a caesarean and she died under the anaesthetic. I had other Standard Poodles, even her litter sister, but the pain I felt was immense.

I tell you this story so you will realise that although Standard Poodles are considered easy whelpers because of the puppies' narrow heads, this is not always the case. Things can, and do, go wrong. Every litter is a risk. If you still want to breed after serious thought, then I hope that the following pages will help you do so wisely. There are many things to consider before taking the risk of producing your litter.

DECIDING TO BREED
If you are an amateur you must consider whether you will be able to sell the puppies. Do not think you can just put an advertisement in the local paper and they will all fly away. Whole litters of pups have come on to the Rescue because novice breeders have not been able to sell them. Do you have time to rear a litter? If you go out to work, then the answer is no. Do you have the space for whelping and to house anything up to twelve puppies until they are ten to twelve weeks old? Are you in a position to socialise the puppies from the age of about four weeks?

If the answer to all these questions is yes, then think, why is it that you want to breed from this bitch? What has she that is of such virtue that you wish to hand it down for posterity? And, above all, does your bitch have such a sweet and confident nature, such a wonderful temperament, that you know she will make a good mother, passing her precious nature through to her young?

THE BROOD BITCH
Standard Poodle bitches generally come into season, or reach sexual maturity at about eight to ten months. Some bitches

are as late as 15-16 months before their first show. There is no rule about this. However, the fact that the bitch has reached sexual maturity in no way implies she is ready to have a litter. No Standard Poodle bitch should be mated before the age of two years. Two-and-a-half years is better. Breeding on two consecutive seasons must be avoided. A litter once a year is more than enough for a bitch, and depending on how many puppies she produces in a litter, three or four litters is the most she should ever have. I have had four litters from a bitch who produced four pups in each litter. Some bitches have 12 puppies in one litter. Such a large litter is a terrible strain on the bitch even with supplementary feeding and early weaning.

Seasons, or heats, usually appear every six months. Prior to a season a bitch may be a bit off-colour and even grumpy – pre-menstrual tension. Sometimes she will go off her food a week before the show, sometimes the appetite is increased. Again, there is no hard and fast rule. All bitches are different. The vulva, or external genital, will swell, a discharge will follow, being quickly replaced with blood. Usually this blood is bright red at the onset, darkening after several days, and may subside to a pale pink or watery straw colour. Here again, there is no rule. Seasons vary. The first season is very often the heaviest the bitch will ever have.

About eight days into the season the bitch will start to be sexually playful with other dogs and bitches. She is not ready for mating yet, under normal circumstances. She may flirt, but if she is introduced to a stud dog she will growl, jump away from him, and may even bite him – or you, if you try to force the issue.

Am. Ch. Blue Skies Whirlaway with her puppies: Breeding is a big responsibility and should not be undertaken lightly.
Photo: Missy Yuhl.

From her eleventh day the bitch will become more receptive to a mate or stud dog. Again, this will vary and you could have to wait until her sixteenth or so day. Of course, the nuisance for the owner is that you may have to travel a long way to mate the bitch. Then, when she meets the dog and it becomes obvious by her aggression she is not ready for him, another trip will have to be made. When I was less well acquainted with my bitches, I once took a bitch back to a stud dog three times, covering hundreds of miles. I usually get it right first time now. The most usual time for mating is at about twelve or thirteen days.

From the eighteenth day, when the ova (egg cells) are discharged from the

117

ovaries, the receptivity of the bitch is diminished. She may still smell attractive to males but will repulse their advances – maybe! Again, there is no one hard-and-fast rule covering a bitch's reproduction system.

SELECTING A STUD DOG

Many people do not understand line-breeding, in-breeding and cross-breeding. Line breeding produces most of our top winning show dogs. At a quick assessment, if your bitch has several ancestors in common in a three or four-generation pedigree, she will be line-bred. In-breeding, in short, is sister to brother etc. and should be avoided at all costs. Out-crossing is where there is no connection between relatives at all. This may be done if there is a bad fault to eradicate. If you are unsure about what to do, show your pedigree to an experienced breeder, who will be able to help.

Choose a stud dog with great care. Just because a dog is a Champion it does not mean he will suit your bitch And do not assume that because he has long ears and your bitch has short ears this will be rectified in the resulting litter. The puppies will not all be born with long ears! Breeding is not that simple. One needs to select carefully to achieve good balance.

To find a stud that you think will suit your bitch, go to the shows, and look at the dogs, including the ones that keep coming second and third as well as the winners. Ask questions. For example, what has the dog produced when mated to bitches with a similar pedigree to your bitch? Make sure the dog you choose complements your bitch. If she is apricot in colour you will not want to use a white dog and lose your colour, no matter how glorious he is. If your bitch is cream or white it is disastrous to use that brown you have a passion for. Remember posterity. Be known for breeding only the best. Even if the first generation of brown/white breeding does not produce freaks, down the line the whites and creams will have pink or liver noses and eye rims etc. I hope you, by now, love this breed enough to want to preserve its virtues. Know your pedigree. Know the stud dog's pedigree. Ask about the colours where they are not stated. Check on the earlier chapter on colour breeding.

Just because a dog has the title of Champion, this does not signify that it will necessarily be a better dog to serve your bitch than a non-Champion. There

Am. Can. Ch. Lemerle Travellin' Lite: A top producer in the US, sire of Am. Ch. Lemerle French Silk.

Downey Photography.

have been many extremely high-quality dogs that have not been Champions. Not everybody has the money, the energy, or the drive to sustain the amount of exhibiting required to make a good dog a Champion. So it is a case of correct matching and – a lot of luck. Do try to produce even, top-quality litters. Above all, temperament must be the prime consideration. And, of course, your bitch must be in pristine condition at the time of mating. She should be wormed, tested for SA and blood-tested for Von Willebrands – see the chapter on inherited diseases.

To go into the science of genetics is beyond the scope of a book of this type. Simplified, the male and female carry the genes inherited from their forefathers. Many breeders do not fully understand the complexities of genetics, but they know, from years of experience, and from knowing the dogs within a pedigree, what the mix of a certain dog to a certain bitch is likely to produce. If your bitch has a fault such as a very light eye, by all means choose a stud for her that has darker eyes; however, if both their ancestors had light eyes that is what you will probably get. If the ancestors had dark eyes you could be on a winner. Half-and-half will produce likewise. Look for balance of temperament, quality and good health.

OWNING A STUD DOG

What has your male got that is of such virtue you feel he has a contribution to make to posterity? Ask yourself this question, and answer it honestly before you offer your dog's services as a stud. A dog reaches sexual maturity at around eight months, and is then capable of mating a bitch at any time, day or night, throughout the year.

The sperm-producing organs (testes) descend into the scrotum of the male at birth, from within the body cavity. Two descended testicles must be present for a male to be 'entire'. Where one or both of the testes fail to descend, this is a condition known as cryptorchidism. Commonly, if only one testicle descends the dog is known as a monorchid. If neither descends he is called a cryptorchid. A monorchid is a fertile animal, but should never be bred from. A chryptorchid is sterile. When one testicle is retained in the body it can become cancerous. Castration, when the lost testicle will be located and removed, together with the one descended, should be seriously considered.

The best time for a potential stud dog to have his first mating is around a year old. The first time it is best to use him on an experienced, receptive bitch, one that has had a litter. This will build his confidence. If an immature bitch is brought for the dog's first stud and she snaps at him, it may well put him off the job altogether. Not all males are so randy they are oblivious about being presented with a screaming, objecting bitch. Some dogs in fact, are not interested in sex at all! Others are so keen they are almost impossible to live with, trying to mate everything in sight, be it chair, human or dog. The best solution for an over-sexed pet dog is castration, to save him from constant frustration and trauma. Hopefully, the very sexy stud dog will settle after he has served a few bitches.

Until your stud dog has produced a litter he is not 'proved'. You can hardly expect a fee for his services until he is proved. It is customary to offer the dog's first stud free of charge, or accept a nominal fee once the resulting litter has arrived. Once he is proved, the normal fee for a Champion is roughly that of the price of a puppy. Less well-known dogs are often considerably cheaper.

The ethics of offering a stud must be considered. Can the owner of the bitch sell the puppies? Are you prepared to help? Is the bitch of sufficient quality to breed from? Is she in good enough health condition? Can the owner of the bitch afford the litter? Do they have room to house the pups? Ask yourself these questions before agreeing to a stud. Please be vigilant and preserve the good name of the Standard Poodle.

Lastly, it is advisable to test the potential stud dog for inherited diseases before offering his services. Stud dogs are invariably blamed for everything that goes wrong with a litter. Although testing does not guarantee freedom from all disease for life, at the time of mating you should be offering a clear dog. Even if you do not care enough about the breed to worry about posterity, the risk of court proceedings are too high these days to ignore. See Chapter 9 for information on inherited diseases for advice on testing.

THE MATING

Usually, the owner of the bitch will take her along to visit the stud dog. The dog and bitch have a quick chat, then a mating takes place and while the 'tying' occurs the owners sit on the floor drinking tea and having a good chat. However, we will look further into this service.

A little consideration shown towards the bitch goes a long way. Firstly, she must be of an even nature and a good standard of quality. Worming advice will have been sought and dispensed with by the vet. The bitch will be clean, healthy and certainly free from parasites, which include ear-mites, that would certainly spread to the puppies. After travelling, and before the introduction to the dog, do give your bitch time to have a little freedom to exercise and to relieve herself. Many a mating has been resisted when the bitch needs to go to the toilet.

It is not always easy to decide if your bitch is ready for mating if you are a novice. Generally speaking, a bitch is extremely encouraging to a dog, practically shoving her rear in his face, even trying to get on top of him when she is ready for mating. For some reason of her own, a bitch may refuse to have one dog service her while, moments later, will happily mate with a different dog. This is rare, but it has happened. One can only sympathise! What to do when the bitch is definitely ready for mating but strenuously resists the service is, perhaps, a difficult question. Personally, I cannot force mate my bitches. I have only owned one bitch that refused adamantly to mate, so I did not mate her. Some may call me soft, but when it is normal for bitches to be as 'sexy' as they can be when they are ready to mate, to have one that is so opposed to it seems suspicious to me.

Most bitches and stud dogs are happy to perform in front of an audience, provided that they are not interfered with too much. I would not leave any of my bitches to be mated out of my sight for any reason at all. Normally the bitch is far happier to have her owner around. She could be quite upset to be deserted by her owner. I do not know of any stud dog owner of Standard Poodles that would expect the owner of a bitch not to be present at a mating.

Some people consider it necessary to use a little Vaseline on the vulva of the bitch to lubricate her. I have tried this once but really prefer not to interfere. Certainly hands must be clean, or an infection could get under way which might wreak havoc with the resulting litter. The membrane of a maiden bitch will be broken by the stud dog; this is much more preferable to having people inserting fingers into sacred places.

A certain amount of foreplay will take place before the stud dog decides to climb on top of the bitch. At this time, with a maiden bitch, it may be beneficial to hold the collar, or her head, in both hands to control a last-minute panic when the dog finally penetrates her. Mostly, bitches are perfectly amenable and stand quite still while the stud dog mates her. Sometimes, once he has turned and is standing beside her, she will almost fall asleep while the tie takes place. Occasionally, a bitch may scream with excitement once the dog has penetrated her and may wriggle. It is imperative that the owner speaks quietly to her and calms her down. She will soon do this. The tie is a procedure that does not always take place, but a litter can still result. However, this is unusual. This tie can take from ten minutes to up to an hour. The more usual time is 15 to 20 minutes.

After the mating has taken place, take the bitch into another room, or put her back into your car, ready for her journey home. Normally, she will sleep heavily for half-an-hour or so making contented little groans.

THE IN-WHELP BITCH
After the mating has taken place it is usual for a bitch to curl up and sleep heavily, especially if there is a long journey home in the car. Within a day or two you can normally tell whether the bitch has conceived. Often they have a dreamy look in their eyes and they may sleep a little bit more. Very slight temperament changes often occur with the newly-pregnant bitch. As the pregnancy progresses into the third week the bitch may have morning sickness. She will refuse food when she is feeling queasy. This may last for a week or so. Some bitches lose their appetite altogether at this stage, which is a bit nerve-racking on the owner.

During the early stages of pregnancy it is quite unnecessary to give the bitch extra food, assuming she is fed a good diet to begin with. Later, at seven to eight weeks, the in-whelp bitch may start asking for more food, and it is better to feed in smaller quantities now, perhaps three or four meals a day instead of the usual two. There is no need to feed additives other than those provided in the normal diet.

You may well find that the bitch has her own ideas about food during pregnancy. I once had a bitch who completely refused everything I offered her, apart from black tripe, throughout her whole pregnancy. This bitch had always had a tremendous appetite, so to find her suddenly so fussy and so adamant when I was wanting her to eat what I thought was good for her, was most disconcerting. However, she produced and reared, with an abundance of milk, five super puppies. When the pups where five weeks old she reverted back to her normal eating habits virtually overnight! The next time I mated her I was expecting trouble. She was totally different for this second pregnancy – the only thing she would not contemplate was cow's milk, yet she loved evaporated. I have learned to go along with pregnant bitches' fads and fancies.

Some bitches are very protective while

they are pregnant. They should be pampered somewhat to make them feel special and secure. Exercise is good and should be fairly normal to begin with. As the pregnancy progresses strenuous exercise, such as the constant throwing of a ball, should be restricted. Walking is good.

At about five weeks into the pregnancy you may notice a broadening in the pregnant bitch's loins and her breasts will become firmer and larger. She may have a clear discharge from her vulva for a few days about this time.

PREPARING FOR WHELPING

The bitch is in whelp for nine weeks (62 or 63 days). Be prepared from fifty-eight days onwards. You will have her whelping quarters ready, in your bedroom or somewhere close by. A large box, about four feet by four feet is good, and about three foot high on three sides and about one foot at the front. This allows her easy access while giving her full security. The box should be an inch or so off the floor to prevent draughts, and lined with vet-bed or something similar, which can easily be changed each day and washed and dried quickly.

Have ready some clean, dry towels to dry the puppies if necessary. Sometimes the bitch may be busy with another puppy coming while the one just born is still wet. In this case wrap the puppy in a towel and rub well. You can do this with the puppy still close to the dam; do not take it right away – and return it to mum the moment she nudges you or the puppy.

Some bitches give obvious signs that their litter is on the way. They scratch the carpet, and try to dig holes in your bed if they can get to it. They dig holes in the garden, pant a lot, whine, go off their food twenty-four hours before whelping, and sometimes get extremely impatient with the other dogs and children. You must not chastise a bitch for any of this behaviour. Better to put her into her whelping quarters and either sit with her, reading a good book on whelping, or keep popping in to check on her. She will sleep heavily in between her frantic times and may want to pop outside frequently to relieve herself, to reduce the pressure as the pain increases.

GIVING BIRTH

If you watch your bitch closely you will see the first labour pain, a ripple down the length of her spine. As the labour develops the bitch will curl up, turn around and flop down, sighing. She will then begin the progress of contracting more seriously. Having got to this stage, if the contractions are coming quickly and no water bag has appeared for two to three hours, consult your vet. It is always better to be safe rather than sorry. All litters are nerve-racking, but the first is the worse.

The bitch will produce a water sac, or shoot out a watery discharge before each puppy. She will quickly lick this away. Each puppy is born in a sac and is attached to a placenta. The bitch will normally tear the sac with her teeth, chump on the cord to detach it from the placenta and eat the placenta, the afterbirth. This is perfectly natural and the nutrients in the placenta, which is used during pregnancy to nourish the puppy, can only do her good. These nutrients are high in natural calcium easily assimilated by the bitch and are said to prevent Eclampsia, which is discussed later.

If a novice bitch has been agitated and distressed for some time before the arrival of her first puppy, she may be a bit disorientated when the puppy arrives, and need a few moments before she realises what she must do. In this case, do not be forceful. Without removing the puppy from the bitch, use your clean fingers to tear the sac. Hold the puppy downwards to prevent it from choking on the fluid from the sac, clean out its mouth with the clean towel, then if the bitch is still not interested – she may be in pain with another puppy coming – dry the puppy vigorously with the towel. Sometimes a novice bitch is more relaxed and able to cope after her second puppy is born. It is essential that you remain calm and sensible at this stage. Have the radio or the television on. Do not try to force the issue. Standard Poodles make very good mothers, assuming they have been reared correctly and have a suitable temperament for breeding, and that they are not unwell, and are not too immature.

Puppies naturally seek their mother's milk quite soon after their arrival. Provided they are warm, they will snuggle up to each other and make little contented noises. If they groan or cry, they are either cold or hungry. There is a difference in the sound of a complaining, cold or hungry pup from one that is disgruntled because its mother has moved or its litter mate has disturbed it. The rattling wail of the abnormal pup is heart-rending.

FEEDING THE DAM
During whelping mum can have drinks of full-cream milk with glucose. After whelping she can be offered food such as chicken and rice. Bitches vary; sometimes they will eat a large meal immediately after whelping, sometimes it is several hours before they begin to eat normally.

Janavons Goldilocks with her newborn puppies: Most Standard Poodle bitches will take motherhood in their stride.

For the first couple of weeks, the mother will see to the puppies' needs, feeding them and cleaning them.

If the bitch does not eat after twenty-four hours, take her temperature and consult the vet. As the milk production increases so will the new mum's appetite. She may want six meals a day until her pups are about eight weeks old.

My bitches are offered the following diet:

Early morning	
(5-6am)	Milk, egg, raw chicken wings
Breakfast	Meat and biscuit
Lunch	Milk, piece of cheese

Dinner	Meat, tripe, beef, chicken and biscuit
Supper	Puppy food
Bedtime	Diced bread and butter with milk.

THE FIRST FEW WEEKS

For about two weeks after the birth of her puppies it is better to keep other dogs and children away from the whelping box, unless the bitch is very happy to have them around. Bitches can be very protective with their young and may bite strangers at this time. This is perfectly natural reaction to retain security for her litter. It is up to you to guard the bitch's security; she will soon let you know by her behaviour when she is ready to socialise her litter.

When the pups first arrive the bitch will not want to leave them. It sometimes takes much persuasion to get her to go outside to relieve herself. As time passes by, and when she is ready, feeling happy and secure, she will pop out of her whelping box to see you and the family at odd times. Gradually, as the pups become less demanding, the bitch will spend more and more time out of the box, only staying with the pups for feeding and cleaning. This is natural, and is the natural progression towards weaning. The bitch may want some exercise with her mates at this time. Usually, though, she will sleep with the puppies all night until they are about four or five weeks.

TIME TO SOCIALISE

Once the bitch decides her puppies are quite safe without her standing guard twenty-four hours a day – and this time does vary – then it is safe to assume it is time for grannies and aunts to look at the puppies. This they normally do with great caution to begin with. Older bitches seem to know when this time has come and are keen to have a nuzzle at the litter. By the time the pups are about five weeks old, mum is normally more than happy to allow her family to share the maternal duties of washing. Of course, this does rather depend on the way you have reared your Poodles. I tend to let nature take its course. In the wild, dogs live as families who all look after the young, and their natural instincts are still with them today.

SUPPLEMENTARY FEEDING

If your bitch has a large litter you must supplement the feeding. You will have got a supply of puppy milk from your local stockist before whelping in case of

Do not economise on the size of your whelping box. This one measures 4ft by 4ft.

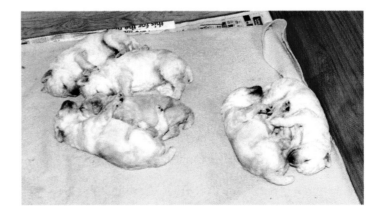

emergencies – some bitches do not have any milk at all. If your bitch has up to six puppies she should cope perfectly well until they are three-and-a-half weeks old, when you can introduce small quantities if fine-minced beef. Extra milk is not normally necessary unless your bitch has very little; thankfully, that is rare.

With more than six puppies, supplements will probably be required into the second or third week. If your poor bitch is unlucky enough to have twelve or so puppies, then you must seriously consider hand-rearing some. Culling is an option I hate to contemplate and have never had to consider. I mate my bitches late, not before fourteen days, and I always get small litters of four or five, which is great for me and the bitch. I have not read of any scientific proof to back this claim, but it works every time for my bitches. A small litter can be thoroughly enjoyed by the bitch, and the breeder has more time to spend on each puppy, checking them over on a daily basis, and getting them used to being handled.

WEANING
I never take my bitches away from their puppies. I feed the puppies with meat twice a day from four weeks, and three times a day from five weeks; their mum keeps them going in-between. Start them off by holding the pup in one hand on your lap and having some fine raw mince in the palm of the other hand. Allow the puppy to sniff this meat and you will be surprised how quickly the pup goes for it. If the pup is not yet hungry it will not stay keen for long. Use only about a teaspoon of meat to begin with and increase as the pup's appetite increases. This intimate dealing with the young puppies will set their temperaments for life.

Even when the puppies are eating solid food they will still feed from their mother as long as she is willing.

HOUSE TRAINING
From about three weeks the puppies can have the front of their whelping box removed and newspaper placed in front of the vet-bed. It never fails to amaze me how soon Standard Poodle puppies come off their bed or blanket to spend a penny. If you have kept them on a clean fresh bed since they were born, they will be clean from habit already.

Weather permitting, the door to the outside world can be left open during the day once the pups are getting active. From about five weeks they will venture to the door and sniff the world. Mum will trot in and out and soon they will follow her. They virtually housetrain themselves in this way, copying mum.

I erect a two foot high pen around the door so that the pups are contained; this allows mum the freedom to jump in and

By seven weeks the puppies are fully weaned and are becoming increasingly independent.
Photo: Eastern Daily Press.

out at her will. The other Standards usually come up to say hello to the pups and have a little play through the fence, or jump over the fence for closer inspection. I consider this to be nature's way of development. There is never any bad feeling between mum and her mates; she has lived with these relations all her life, after all. Strange dogs are something else and should never have this freedom to encroach on the dam's environment.

The worst part of breeding is that all the puppies cannot be kept. Every time I breed a litter I get so upset when the puppies finally have to go to their new homes, that I always say I will not breed any more.

Puppies must be wormed at four, six and eight weeks. I get the preparation from my vet. I do not vaccinate before ten to twelve weeks; some breeders panic and do it far too soon as far as I am concerned. Because of the way my puppies are reared I maintain they have good, natural antibody protection.

Homeopathic nosodes are now being widely used and recommended. Contact the Homeopathic Association for your nearest vet who uses these preparations.

DOCKING AND DEWCLAWS

Standard Poodles are customarily docked at one to three days old, in countries that still allow this. In England we have the Council of Docked Breeds to help us find a suitable vet. Join this helpful organisation when you first decide to have a litter. It is no use waiting until the litter is born and then trying to find a vet who will dock them. Dew claws must be removed at the same time. In America docking is still carried out by breeders because they do not have the same rules as does the UK with regard to docking. Some countries ban docking altogether, while others allow it to be carried out by a vet.

PERSONAL CHOICE

Each breeder will have their own way of

rearing puppies. No doubt we all think our own way to be the best. Luckily I have a husband who is as daft about the dogs as I am, and is quite content to have puppies in the bedroom or wherever. Personally, if I had to keep Standard Poodles in a kennel outside I would not have them. They are born to be people dogs and not a number in Block B!

DEALING WITH PROBLEMS

Uterine inertia: I have never experienced this at first hand but it is a fact that occasionally a bitch may suffer from uterine inertia. The bitch will have very weak contractions, or maybe no contractions at all. The problem here is that for an inexperienced breeder it can be extremely difficult to detect the condition – which could result in a caesarean operation being needed to save the puppies and the dam. It is most unfortunate if this happens with a first litter and it is quite possible for the bitch to die. More experienced breeders will be aware, by signs of mildly different behaviour, that the bitch has actually started to whelp. The only sign may be that the bitch sits upright, pushing into the back of a chair; a slight twist may be seen in her abdomen or just some twitching of the hind leg. A brisk walk in the garden or a bumpy ride to the vet may get the bitch going. Certainly consult your vet if the bitch seems to be hanging on to her puppies. It is always better to be safe rather than sorry.

Puppy stuck in vulva: Sometimes it happens that a puppy is breech-born. If the bitch is not sufficiently stretched the puppy may get stuck half-in and half-out. The bitch will need assistance to produce the puppy. Vaseline can help if the area looks dry, then grasp the puppy's protruding part with a clean, dry towel. When next the bitch contracts, give a gentle, easing tug, downwards, or from side to side. Take care never to pull the puppy out unless the bitch is pushing and contracting. You may severely hurt her. Should you lose hold of the puppy and it disappears back inside the bitch, you may be lucky enough to see it pushed down with the next puppy that is eager to arrive. I do not recommend novice breeders to feel into the vulva for the puppy. This could be dangerous and cause infection. It is wiser to have an experienced breeder with you for your first few litters or consult your vet. You do not want to lose your bitch.

Over-enthusiasm with umbilical cord: It is the most natural thing in the world for a bitch to eat the placenta, the afterbirth. Sometimes, however, a novice bitch may chump through the cord and not know where to stop. You must intervene and tell her to stop. Offer her the mouth or rear of the puppy to lick. Once the cord is dry there is no longer any danger.

Dead-looking pup on arrival: Wipe away moisture from around the mouth and nostrils. Rub vigorously with a dry towel. Massage the puppy between your hands with the head facing downwards. It may take some time – minutes – to revive the pup. Do not give in too easily. Once it has gasped for breath, do keep massaging until the breathing sounds regular. It may be necessary to breathe into the pup's mouth. To do this place your mouth over the puppy's mouth and nostrils and breathe in and out normally for as long as you can without taking your mouth away. This attempt to get the puppy's lungs stimulated can be successful. However, if the pup is dead there is nothing that will stimulate it into breathing.

Puppy not feeding after birth: Puppies normally feed within a very short time of being born. They instinctively seek the milk bar. If a puppy does not feed immediately, or within a short time, be sure to keep it warm. Insert your finger into the roof of the pup's mouth to be sure there is no sign of a fissure. This fissure, called a cleft palate, arises when the bones that make up the roof of the mouth do not fuse properly and leave a gap. Puppies with a severe cleft palate cannot feed properly and soon die. This is a congential abnormality, thankfully rarely seen in Standard Poodles. In fact, I have never actually seen it.

If all seems well there, but the puppy is still not feeding when the others have arrived and are feeding well, then do try to encourage feeding. Gently open the pup's mouth and pop the mother's teat inside it, gently squeezing a drop or two of the milk into the puppy's mouth. If after this, and an hour or so later, the puppy still does not want food, it may well have internal problems. Sometimes puppies such as this can be hand-reared but they invariably die before two weeks. If the puppy is just weak from the whelping, it should soon pick up after a couple of supplementary feeds.

Diarrhoea: The bitch may have very loose motions immediately after whelping. This is perfectly normal and usually lasts about 24 hours. If after 36 hours she is not eating, and feels unusually hot, consult your vet in case infection has set in.

Eclampsia: This is unusual but it does

happen. Sometimes stress will induce this dreadful condition. I once had a bitch that went down with eclampsia within a few hours of having a parvovirus jab. She had to be injected with calcium every day for two weeks. Do not ever ignore the symptoms of eclampsia. This condition, if not treated without delay, is fatal. The symptoms are: extreme restlessness, with the bitch not settling with her litter; the bitch carrying her puppies about in her mouth dementedly; or trying to hide them; or trying to dig a hole in her whelping box, and scattering the puppies. She may shiver, cry, pant and tremble. A sure sign of danger is a distinct changing of the colour of the tongue and a strange, bright stare in her eyes. If left the bitch will collapse and become unconscious. This is caused by the calcium reserves in her body becoming too low. No amount of oral calcium feeding at any stage can prevent or cure this condition. You need a vet without delay.

Mastitis: Occasionally a bitch has too much milk and a build-up can cause severe discomfort. Her teats will swell and be red and hot. It may be necessary to draw off some milk until the puppies are older and requiring more. This condition does not normally last more than a few days, but if the bitch looks very red and is obviously sore with her enlarged teats, then take advice from your vet.

No milk at all: This has happened to one of my bitches. The bitch had a perfect whelping, produced eight lovely puppies and never had a drop of milk. These puppies had to be hand-reared with substitute milk. I fed them every two hours, day and night, for two weeks, then every three hours for a week, then every four hours. At least I had the dam to clean and love the puppies and keep them warm and cosy. To lose a bitch is devastating; not only must you then feed the puppies, you must clean them with cotton wool after each feed, rubbing against their tummies to encourage them to go to toilet, and keeping their mouths clean.

Metritis: This is an infection of the uterus. Symptoms show themselves by a raised temperature, loss of appetite, and an evil-smelling greenish-black discharge. Consult your vet.

Fading puppies: A wailing cry from a puppy indicates serious trouble. There are several theories but no conclusions as to why puppies fade. Sometimes it may be due to infection. It is possible there may be liver shunt or some other deformity. It is heartbreaking to lose one puppy, but to lose a whole litter is devastating to the dam as well as to the breeder. Fading puppy syndrome, or disease, can happen from when the pups are a few days old onwards. An apparently healthy puppy at birth can suddenly look very sick indeed, and die. Then another puppy dies. This can happen through the whole litter. It is believed that the most common factor that causes fading puppy disease is by two types of bacteria; a streptococcus strain and another, known as E. coli (B. coli). However, other factors or viruses can be responsible. Puppies once infected cannot survive. At the very first sign of a puppy looking unwell, not feeding properly, having a messy motion, feeling unduly hot or cold, call the vet in order to be on the safe side.

$\mathcal{9}$ *HEALTH CARE*

On the whole Standard Poodles are tough, healthy dogs. They are creatures of habit, so any change in their personality or behaviour could be a sign of physical or mental distress or pain. Watch your dog carefully if its normal habits and reactions seem altered in any way. If you are concerned, consult an experienced breeder or your vet. Early care and treatment often saves pain, discomfort and expense. Standard Poodles are very sensitive to their owner's behaviour. If you feel sad, at a loss, or pained for any reason, your Standard Poodle will pick this up and may show signs of being off-colour too. Here are the diseases, some of which can be inherited and others that are contracted in various ways, that we need to be concerned about. There are tips about behavioural problems and, finally, how to care for our elderly Poodle.

ADDISON'S DISEASE
Primary Addison's is an auto-immune disease affecting mostly female dogs in middle age. It apparently affects females in a two-to-one ratio over males. It can occur when the adrenal hormone is produced in inadequate amounts, sometimes caused by a tumour, or as a result of a haemorrhage due to certain diseases such as distemper or pyometra. Secondary Addison's can result from a pituitary problem. Early symptoms, including sporadic episodes of diarrhoea, vomiting, loss of appetite and lethargy, can sometimes be missed, as there often is a spontaneous recovery. As the disease progresses the episodes may be more frequent. Depression and diminished kidney function can occur. Addison's is fatal if not diagnosed and treated. Treatment is simple and lifelong and usually consists of the administration of tablets. A simple blood test with a complete blood profile will detect the disease.

ANAL GLANDS
These are glands that are situated either side of the anus. Sometimes bitches just out of season are troubled with blocked glands. Smelly and irritating glands will cause the dog to rub its bottom along on the carpet or grass. This condition is often caused by an inadequate diet lacking in bones. To relieve it, take a

Standard Poodles are tough dogs built on athletic lines, and most will live a long, healthy life.

sheet of kitchen role, place finger and thumb either side of the anus and press in, up and outwards; this will expel the vile-smelling fluid and sometimes a thick, brown substance of a toothpaste-like texture. Raw bones and plenty of exercise should prevent anal glands from becoming troublesome.

BLOAT AND GASTRIC TORSION

This is extremely stressful and serious. It is usually fatal. Bloat probably does occur more commonly in older dogs, six to nine years and onwards, but young dogs have died from it. It affects many deep-chested breeds. The most usual time for bloat onset is between 6pm and midnight. Dietary factors, which appear to increase the risk of the condition occurring, include dogs bolting food, dogs being fed fewer, larger meals per day, and exercise immediately after a meal. Stress factors such as a beating or the fear of other dogs and people, can cause it. A dog with a history of belching is at increased risk. A heavy meal on an empty stomach is never a good idea. Latest research seems to suggest that dogs which are fed a high biscuit diet are more at risk from bloat. Indeed, many dogs which have stolen their way into the biscuit barrel and gorged themselves have, within hours, developed bloat.

Early recognition of bloat is essential to saving the dog's life. The dog looks sad and may cry if you try to move it. The stomach feels hard, with the dog showing obvious signs of abdominal pain. The dog seeks a cold floor to lie on, or will try to hide in a corner, or under the table, showing it is stressed. The stomach may grow large and feel blown out. Surgery must be immediate. If the dog lives through the dreadful trauma of a bout of bloat then be prepared for the condition to reappear. Dogs suffering bloat inevitably have a reoccurrence. If you have the smallest suspicion that a dog has bloat, contact your vet without delay.

131

CANKER

Ear problems are normally caused by mites picked up easily from grass or cats. There will be a brown, waxy, smelly substance in and around the ear. Sometimes red sores and inflammation are obvious. Treat the dog by drying the ear as much as possible with cotton wool; apply Thornit to base of ear, leave for about an hour then remove any of the substance now caked and obvious, apply more Thornit. Treat twice a day for one to five days until the brown begins to clear. A pinch of Thornit in the ear once a week should keep the dog clear of mites for life. Cleaning of the ear can also be done with a mixture of liquid paraffin, one part, to two parts methylated or surgical spirit. Use cotton wool dipped into the solution to keep clean the opening of the ear.

If excess hair needs to be removed from the ear, apply a good pinch of Thornit first. The hair will then come out more easily. All my dogs have hair in their ears; I consider it quite natural and only tease out the excess if necessary. It is a fallacy that hair causes ear trouble. Always have Thornit in your dog's medicine cupboard. Be persistent – mites are! Thornit is purchased – and sent all over the world – from Miss P. Bett, Hall Stables, Thornham, Hunstanton, Norfolk, PE36 6NB.

CONSTIPATION

This is quite unusual in dogs and diet is the most common cause of blame. More roughage in the diet will sort this problem out. Dogs that chew raw bones often excrete firm stools; this is quite natural. Do not feed your dog any cooked bones; these are dangerous and can splinter. Raw bones are natural and good.

COUGHS

All dogs cough occasionally. If your dog has a persistent cough for more than a day or two it is better to be on the safe side of caution and ring your vet. A number of diseases and conditions are associated with cough, some infectious. Some heart diseases cause cough. Kennel cough is a contagious virus contacted from other dogs, kennels etc. This can last for many weeks and is most distressing, with the dog heaving like a child with whooping cough. Often with kennel cough the dog will vomit bile. Some vets advocate treatment with antibiotics, while others leave well alone unless the dog is distressed. When in doubt, consult your vet.

DIARRHOEA

The best way for the dog to rid itself of impurities is through diarrhoea. Many dogs rid themselves of toxins through this natural process; it is therefore not such a good idea to immediately 'bung' the dog up, as this may allow the impurities which the dog is trying to evacuate to invade further into the system. If diarrhoea persists for more than twenty four hours, and is accompanied with a rise in temperature, veterinary help may be required. Blood in the stools should be investigated without delay. One should have a dog thermometer in the first aid kit. It is best to take a dog's temperature before a trip to the vet because the trip itself may cause a slight rise.

ECZEMA

More often than not eczema is caused by an allergy to fleas or mites. There may be red, sore patches, tiny at first, sometimes weeping. The dog may have intense scratching and irritation. The skin may feel very hot. Occasionally eczema can be attributed to an allergy to diet. Cereals are an extremely unnatural substance for a dog, yet they are found (along with additives) in all dry dog food; many dogs are intolerant of them. If you are feeding these foods and your dog has irritations when there is absolutely no sign of inflammation caused by foreign bodies, change the diet to a more natural one.

EYES

Standard poodles rarely inherit eye trouble. Some puppies will have quite watery eyes during the teething period (up to six months). For a white this can be most distressing, because a brown mark will stain the face where the tears overflow. Keep this wiped dry as often as possible. Also the weather, particularly wind, can cause eyes to water. Keep the eyes clean and, once the head has finished growing, the problem should right itself. If it does not come right after the dog is about 13 months, get the eye checked. Excess watering, or fluid, is produced by conjunctivitis. This eye infection will need to be professionally treated. Do try to keep the eyes clean. If you have more than one Standard Poodle you will normally find they will wash each other's eyes every day.

FLEAS AND MITES

In the case of fleas give a good bath in tea-tree shampoo, then spray with a preparation obtained from the vet. Repeat spray in five to seven days, and in ten days, or after every bath. It is advisable to spray the house with house spray from the vet at the same time. Even people who do not own animals have bugs in their fitted carpet.

During hot, dry months, and because of mild winters and today's centrally heated homes, harvest mites, and those tiny, impossible-to-see, rabbit mites, have become more of a problem. It is best to spray the house frequently if you have cats.

For dogs with red, sore spots on their skin, apply Thornit to the area. Sulphur is excellent for cooling and balancing the blood, and it is obtainable from any pharmacy or health shop. Give two tablets every hour for six hours to dogs that are hot and very itchy, then two tablets three times a day until scratching abates. Add sulphur block to drinking water vessels, about one inch broken from a block.

Intense scratching on all parts of the body where there is no evidence of fleas is usually caused by the migration of the ear or rabbit mite, transferring itself to the scurf of the body. This mite is very minute and very mobile; skin scrapings probably will not reveal them. Shampooing seems useless. If you look carefully through the coat (on a dark dog this will have to be intensely) you will find tiny pink or red spots on the skin. When you find these you will have probably found a mite's nest. Dust with Thornit. If scratching continues after dosing a couple of times, your dog may have got into the habit of scratching, which is not an easy habit to break. Mites can easily get under the claws, causing constant licking because of irritation. It is a good idea to dust the toes of such a dog, or put some Thornit into a plastic bag and place the dog's foot inside for a few minutes.

HIP DYSPLASIA

Strenuous exercise before the bones are grown can cause many bone problems, including hip dysplasia although, thankfully, there are very few Standard

Poodles who suffer with this disorder. A very young puppy being constantly pushed into the sitting position may suffer damage, or one that is allowed to run up and down stairs many times a day. If a puppy bunny-hops, this is usually a sign of stress on rear joints. It is essential to restrict exercise to a minimum where bunny-hoping is evident until the dog has grown, and still sometimes after that. Older dogs with joint problems should only have very short, quiet walks.

Bad rearing and feeding probably is responsible for most bone problems At this moment in time there does not seem to be a definite inheritance factor, as two dogs, X-ray cleared, can throw a dog with hip dysplasia, and vice versa. However, some conscientious breeders advocate X-raying.

LUMPS

Injury, abscess, cyst, warts, ulcers, haematoma – there are many reasons why your Standard Poodle may develop a lump. If your dog knocks himself, a swelling may appear and disappear within a few days and the dog seems none the worse. A more serious injury can cause internal bleeding which develops into a lump. This may need veterinary treatment. Warts and cysts often appear in older dogs, along with fatty-tissue lumps. Whenever a cyst or wart looks suspicious, seek veterinary help. Dogs that are made to sleep on concrete or a hard floor will develop lumps on their joints.

PHANTOM PREGNANCY

A bitch may display signs of pregnancy even if she is not carrying a litter. One or two months after the season, and varying in severity, the bitch shows signs of nervousness, panting, morning sickness, digging a nest (in carpet, garden or otherwise). She may carry toys about in her mouth and nurse them in her bed. She may produce milk. Probably something like seventy percent of bitches have phantom, or false, pregnancies. Some will nurse an orphaned litter at this time. Treat the bitch as normal and allow plenty of exercise. After a few weeks she will return to normal if you do not pander to her.

PYOMETRA

This is an accumulation of large amounts of fluid in the uterus. Usually this condition occurs four to eight weeks after the bitch has been in season. She may start to drink excessively. She may want to spend a lot more pennies, sometimes leaking in the house, although she has never done this before. Depression, often with a raised temperature, shows. Abdominal pain occurs, and often a reddish-brown or murky discharge from the vulva can be seen. The bitch may continually clean herself around this area. This condition is serious. Sometimes it is fatal. Consult your vet if you are the slightest bit suspicious. Removal of the uterus and ovaries is normally required to safeguard the bitch's life.

RINGWORM

This is a fungal skin infection which can attack cats and humans as well as dogs. Each can pass it to the other. The skin has a distinctive whitish ring just beneath the skin. Cut away the hair and apply ointment made especially for this condition.

SEBACEOUS ADENITIS

This is a distressing skin condition that is

more common in some countries than in others, it seems. It is important to be aware of this disease in lines you are contemplating breeding from. Many breeds are affected with SA, some with milder forms than others. In some cases clinical signs are mild scaling and minimal hair loss. At its worse this disease can be severe, with secondary bacterial infection. The coat may be generally dry and difficult to groom, with more tangles forming, and with a loss of coat during routine grooming. Hair may have small scales attached to the base. In some more advanced cases there may be significant loss of hair progressing from the head and withers to the whole of the trunk. Diagnosis is by the examination of a skin biopsy. Small sections of skin are removed with the aid of a local anaesthetic by a vet and are sent to a veterinary pathologist with knowledge of the disease.

Treatment is based on controlling secondary infections, together with an attempt to help the dog grow a resemblance of a normal coat. The application of oils, such as baby oil, or bath oil such as tea-tree oil, are considered helpful in the control of the disease; also the use of fatty acids such as Evening Primrose oil. If you are worried about your Standard Poodle's coat and your vet is not acquainted with SA, contact the Health Officer of the Standard Poodle Club (from any country) and you will be advised on referrals. All Standard Poodles should be tested for SA before being bred from.

SPAYING AND CASTRATION
Both female and male dogs are frequently altered to prevent unwanted pregnancy. If you have a male and female living together in your home it is quite cruel to allow the bitch to come into season once the dog has reached sexual maturity at about six to nine months. The dog will become frantic even when the two are parted. It is kinder by far to have the bitch spayed or the dog castrated, or both. They must be of mature age before they are altered. For the bitch, this is after her first season (bitches are spayed eight to ten weeks after a season, because this is the best time hormone-wise). Dogs are best seen to between ten and twenty-two months of age, or at any time after that. Pet males are certainly less distressed once they are castrated. This does not change their personality except to make them more gentle. Two males living together and starting to display challenging behaviour are best castrated without delay. Bitches can sometimes get temperamental before a season and when coming out of season. If your normally sweet-natured girl gets this way it may be kinder to have her spayed. Altered dogs and bitches cannot be shown without Kennel Club consent.

STINGS
Wasp and bee stings can be severe and dangerous when the face, mouth or neck are affected. If the sting is visible, pull it out with a pair of tweezers. Apply soothing ointment or meat tenderiser. The dog may need veterinary treatment in some cases.

TAKING THE TEMPERATURE
The normal temperature for a dog is 101.5° F. Shake the thermometer and insert the bulb end one inch into the rectum, leave it there for one minute, then remove and read. Care should be taken by an inexperienced person when taking a temperature; accidents can

happen and thermometers have been known to break in the rectum. Unless you are competent in these matters, get somebody to assist you.

TEETH

If your dog is allowed lots of raw, meaty bones it is most unlikely that you will ever need to scale its teeth. Bones also do a good job on dirty teeth and they are far less expensive than the vet! Dogs that live on a diet of soft tinned food and no hard biscuit will accumulate scale on their teeth. If this scale is not removed by bone chewing or with a tooth scaler – and in drastic cases the vet will be required – then tooth decay will result. Your dog will have smelly breath and may lose some of its teeth.

VACCINATIONS

There are some top veterinary immunologists who tell us that annual vaccinations for viral diseases are unnecessary, even harmful to our dogs. Yet we are encouraged by others to take the precaution of annual vaccinations. No wonder we may be confused.

It is essential for a puppy to be in perfect health before vaccination. Research has shown that a reaction to vaccination can lead to inflammation of the brain, which in turn can lead to certain allergies, to colitis, epilepsy, eating disorders, skin problems and so on. More research is needed and data is being collected. At this time it is extremely difficult, in some cases of disease and illness, to be certain whether or not the immunity system has been in some way damaged by the excess use of vaccination. Do not blame breeders for everything that goes wrong. Some things are out of our hands.

Because of the problems breeders have

been faced with over disease and health problems, which are escalating but do not seem to have a genetic sequence, much research is being done, particularly in America, to try to distinguish the source of these problems. The way in which we vaccinate is seriously suspicious. Some people suggest that there do seem to be sound grounds for believing that the parvovirus vaccine, when given in conjunction with other diseases, can suppress the immune system. Any dog which has heavily stained teeth has more than likely suffered sub-acute distemper from the vaccination. Nosodes are an alternative to vaccination and are thought by many to be far safer than the vaccination system given today. More information about nosodes can be obtained from your nearest homeopathic vet, or from Homeopathic Societies.

Another method which some find is proving very successful is having the vaccination given over a longer period – six or more separate injections with no closer time than two weeks between. Currently the popular system of two or three doses is used with only a two-week time gap in between.

Many breeders who have experienced problems in dogs which can be related to vaccination must take this research seriously. If you have suffered with a dog with bloat, seizures, stained teeth, skin problems – immunity breakdown – there is no way to be sure that the problem did not start from overloading the immune system with multiple diseases.

Puppies over ten to twelve weeks do need some form of immunisation. It is only right to warn owners that there is the possibility of a reaction. However, the risk is said to be small and the devastation which would take place if there were no vaccines is too horrific to contemplate. Imagine the world with no rabies vaccine. In the UK we are lucky very rarely ever to see this disease. Other countries are not so lucky. We have to try to weight the balance.

VON WILLEBRANDS

This is the most common bleeding disorder in animals. Unfortunately it is an inherited disease. Signs to watch for are recurrent bleeding: gastrointestinal; urinary tract; nose bleeds; lameness (bleeding from the joints); prolonged bleeding in season; blood blisters. Thankfully, diagnosis is by a simple blood test. Vigilant breeders have their Standard Poodles tested for this disease before breeding from a dog or bitch.

WORMS

With the panic in the last few years, blown up out of all proportion, some poor dogs got dosed with poisonous vermifuge so frequently it is a wonder they did not die of poisoning. All responsible breeders worm their dams and their puppies, and will give you a worming certificate with the dates of when the doses were given and what preparation was used, with the date of the next worming. All new puppy owners should insist on receiving such information. Unless there is evidence of worms, such as segments of tape worm around the anus or in the stool, a dull lifeless coat, lose of weight, or an unpleasant odour on breath and skin, there is no need to worm more than once or twice a year. If you are unsure, a test of faeces can be done by your vet before administration of unnecessary poisons.

A FEW DO'S AND DON'TS

DO leave clean, fresh water with added sulphur for drinking at all times.
DO feed at least twice a day.
Do feed after walks.
Do go for walks.
Do groom your Poodle and have it regularly trimmed.
Do socialise your puppy from the start.
Do allow your puppy plenty of rest.
Do start training and socialising classes early.
Do give raw meaty bones to chew.
Do get yourself a kind, reputable vet.
Do take a plastic bag on walks to clear up after your dog.
Don't leave your Poodle alone all day, every day.
Don't leave your Poodle in the car in warm weather.
Don't give your dog cooked bones.
Don't expect your new puppy to understand your foreign language.
Don't breed without serious consideration.
Don't wait six months before you have your Poodle trimmed.
Don't leave your Poodle until it is six months old before you socialise it.

THE ELDERLY STANDARD POODLE

Probably the saddest thing about old age is that it creeps up on a dog and, sometimes, we are not fully aware of it. As time passes by, that boisterous puppy we were sure would never settle down to be a calm commendable friend seems suddenly to have developed lumps. We are astonished when one day normal food is refused, walks become more effort, lying in longer and longer in the morning becomes a habit. Suddenly we are aware that when we call there is little response, and movement has slowed to a sniffing pace. Blindness has crept in. Some Standard Poodle owners, with

Jane pictured at sixteen years of age: The veteran deserves special consideration.

their total idolisation of a pet, can easily cause that treasured pet stress by refusing to accept the inevitable. The dog is old.

Eyes deteriorate, as does hearing, as the dog ages. Muscles lose their elasticity and strength, bones are more brittle, and sometimes painful. In old age it is essential to take notice of tell-tale signs of stress. Shorten those daily walks if your dog becomes stiff after the normal walk. Little and often is more beneficial. Old dogs who have been used to going for walks all their life hate to have their routine changed, but continuing that same routine may cause stress to old joints. It is essential to reach a compromise. Walking is good at any age. Moderate the walks as age becomes apparent.

Diet may need to be altered for the elderly dog. Some old dogs may still relish chewing on raw meaty bones but they seem to find eating and digesting biscuit more difficult. Choose a diet that is easy for the older dog to cope with; soak the biscuit, or add crushed oats to meat along with the vegetables; try puppy food on that elderly dog which seems to have lost its appetite.

Check the mouth for bad teeth. Dogs not having had raw bones throughout their life will certainly have decaying teeth in old age. Some teeth may need to be removed by the vet in order to prevent poison being assimilated by the dog. Elderly dogs need more peace and quiet. They need their own space where they can relax and not be disturbed when asleep. However, old dogs who have spent their lives with a family hate to be locked away. They should be allowed their own space where they can keep an eye on the world as it passes by.

Sickness in the elderly Standard Poodle is distressing. Lumps and bumps may suddenly appear from nowhere. Fatty tissue lumps often grow under the skin on the body; a dog may have one or two. Sometimes these hard but fluid-feeling lumps are found on the legs. These fatty tissue lumps do not seem to cause any problems with most dogs and are best left alone.

Tumours in the stomach are more disconcerting and need veterinary advice to identify them and to help decide on the best course of action. Bitches can grow mammary growths that need to be removed before they become too large. Again, consultation with the vet is a necessity.

On the whole Standard Poodles are pretty healthy dogs if raised properly. The odd dog will have trouble no matter what. It is inevitable. Standard Poodles tend to live for at least twelve years. It is not unusual for them to live up to fourteen or sixteen years of age. I have heard of one living for twenty-one years. But do not hesitate, when you know in your heart of hearts that the time has come, to put your friend to sleep. Do not prolong suffering.

10 LEADING BRITISH KENNELS

Some kennels have been at the forefront of Standard Poodles in the show ring for many years. Other smaller and more restricted breeders have produced many good dogs. It is impossible to include all the kennels in the country so I have tried to select those who have consistently produced quality Standard Poodles. There are some smaller, young kennels of Standard Poodles who are now beginning to make their presence felt by producing good dogs. I hope they will continue to grow from strength to strength and we will see them in an update to this book in the coming years.

Because the Champion title in Britain is so difficult to attain amid the large entries and persistently good quality dogs in Standard Poodles, many excellent dogs have failed to gain the Champion title that they may well deserve. It must be said that not all owners have the resources, the time, or the energy and the total dedication required to campaign a dog to its title. Standard Poodles are about a lot more than owning a Show Champion. However, to have bred one Champion is a credit to a kennel, to have

bred several over many generations shows true dedication and deserves great credit. Show entries in Britain are usually well over the hundred. In 1986 I judged at the British Utility Breeds Association and was honoured to draw a world entry of 299. To this date that world record stands. I am very proud of it.

It must be said that those people who breed colours are often at a disadvantage against those breeders who breed and show black Standard Poodles. I am not sure why judges do not understand colour, but I have always had coloured Poodles – white, cream, blue, silver, brown – and I cannot imagine life without colour. To gain a title with an apricot or a blue or a silver or a brown is a fantastic achievement which deserves noting.

The Standard Poodle club of Great Britain was born in 1965. In April of that year the founder members elected as their Hon. Secretary Mr R. Jenkins, with Mrs M. Skeaping as Chairman. Over thirty years later the Standard Poodle Club of Great Britain is still the only Club of this size and it plays an important role in the education and welfare of the Standard Poodle throughout the world.

KENNELS (A-Z)

BALNOBLE (Brown)
Anne Beswick's foundation bitch Vicmars Legacy of a Legend, a black, which I mentioned in the chapter on the origins of the Standard Poodle, produced the all-time great Ch. Vicmars Balnoble Royale, which was voted Judges' Choice of all-time great Standards in the *Kennel Gazette*. Anne imported, from Susan Frazer in Canada, Bibelots Dreams Come True which was mated to Royale and produced Ch. Balnoble Play It Again Sam. Next came Ch. Balnoble Golly Miss Molly, out of a sister to Balnoble Royale, Misty Miss Christy, and sired by the imported black Ch. Montravia Acadia Nevermore Neville.

A blue dog Bel Tor On With The Show came from the USA and was mated to Molly. A bitch from this litter was mated to Ch. Supernova Smitty at Balnoble and produced a Brown which was to change Anne's life. With the challenge of campaigning and making up this most difficult colour came joy and addiction. Anne is now totally devoted to Browns. Her latest is the young bitch Balnoble One More Dream. On the international circuit was the winning Int. Ch. Springett Beau Bedazzle – a dog of the year for Scandinavia. Meanwhile in South Africa Ch. Balnoble Brigadier Gerald was making a name for himself. Another top winning bitch from this line was Balnoble Bracken Tweed, who was campaigned and owned by Kim and Betty Sillito.

DORVALLE (Apricots)
Dawn and Peter Little purchased their first Standard Poodle, Jackwyn Caramel Prelude, in 1975. In 1977 Alpenden Evening Sunshine was purchased from Mrs Vivienne Kellard with the intention of developing a breeding line of apricot Standard Poodles. The Dorvalle affix was granted in 1977 and is based on Dawn's two Christian names, Dawn and Valerie. Jackwyn Caramel Prelude was mated, but complications in whelping took her life. Her orphaned puppies were hand-reared and the first Dorvalle showdog, Dorvalle Caramel Legacy, emerged. He obtained his Junior Warrant and a Reserve CC, which was the first awarded to this kennel. He and his daughter Dorvalle Caramel Delight JW, were a noted brace in apricots and won a number of Championship awards.

Ch. Balnoble Venture To Cognac.

Dorvalle boast a total of seven home-bred Junior Warrant winners in apricot. The first Dorvalle Champion was born in 1988, Champion Dorvalle Dancing Caramel JW, who gained her title in 1988 and was only the second apricot to achieve this status in 23 years. Her son, Dorvalle Danse Du Feu, attained his Junior Warrant and has won two Reserve Challenge Certificates.

FRENCHES (Apricot, Silver)
Rita Price Jones, who featured in the chapter on the origins of the breed, no longer breeds but she has played a significant part in Standard Poodles. Her kennel started in the early 1940s, the first sire being Champion Vulvan Champagne Darcy. This kennel has produced 32 Champions and won many Best in Shows.

GROOMAR (White, Black)
Margery Cleaver had her first Standard in 1969, Burntoak Darrin. She made up her first Champion in 1972, Vulcan Crystal Clear. Her first home-bred Champion was Groomar Crystal Rock. Other Champions bred by Margery are Captains Lady at Malibu, Surely Supernova, Groomar Sea Breeze, Groomar Chrystal Rock, Groomar White Bird, Groomar Mixed Blessings, Groomar On With The Show at Highla and Hi Look Me Over I'm Groomar, who is the sire of many top winning dogs and Champions. These have been produced from just one litter every two years or so.

HIGHLA (Cream, Black, Blue)
Ann Rawlingson started her kennel in 1957 having had an association with the breed since 1956 when she began training at the Vulcan kennels under the tutelage of Shirley Walne. The affix Highla, was given to Ann by Shirley Walne. It came into being before the Second World War and can be found in Standard Poodle pedigrees from that period. The foundation stock consisted of Vulcan Champagne Anemone, who lived to the ripe old age of 21! Then came Vulcan Champagne May Lily and Vulcan Champagne Candida. These were followed later by Vulcan Escorts Honour (imported from Sweden), Vulcan Champagne Admirer, Vulcan Champagne May Duke, and Vulcan Champagne Charlie. For many years Ann worked hard to establish a quality line of Apricots. Ann bred the influential sire Vulcan Champagne Solid Gold whose name features in so many of the apricots of today. The blue Ch. Twin Tops Conversation Piece is one of Ann's favourite dogs, an import from Sweden who has sired many excellent dogs and Champions, including the winning black bitch Ch. Highla Indyanna Hits Malibu. Twin Tops was a Best of Breed winner at Crufts centenary in 1991. He also sired the bitch Ch. Highla Das Es All With Groomar, a Crufts ticket winner. The black Ch. Hi Look Me Over I'm Groomar has proved himself to be an influential sire of blacks and browns.

JANAVONS (White, Blue)
We registered this affix in 1965 and bred our first litter the following year. We were more interested in Obedience at that time and ring showing did not come until later. Two bitches were purchased from the Vulcan kennels, granddaughters of Champion Vulcan Champagne Damissin – Vulcan Heaven Blest and Vulcan Heaven Knows. After some success in the show ring, both were mated, in different years, to Champion

*Ch. Janavons
Pollyanna: Best in
Show SPC Ch. Show
1984.*

Photo: Diane Pearce.

Blue Balthazar, a son of Champion Vicmars Balnoble Royale. Both produced a Champion. The white, Champion Janavons Daughter of Blest, was hand-reared from birth when her dam died during a caesarean. She become a very popular and much-loved bitch. After winning her first CC she then went on to take the Group at WELKS; she was featured on the cover of the *American Gazette*, and chosen for the cover of Shirley Walne's book.

The second Champion, a dog who is featured in many pedigrees of blues and silvers, was Champion Janavons Midnight Blue. Next came Champion Blue Angel and Int. Fin. Swed. Champion Yanky Doodle Dandy and Int. Fin. Swed. Ch. Janavons Ballerina. Their dam, Janavons Angel Delight, produced three Champions from a litter of five. The sire of this litter was Champion Dassin Diablo, an American import. The other two puppies were not shown, but one produced Champion Janavons Pollyanna who won Best in Show at the SPC Championship Show in 1984. The black Janavons Midnight Gold won Best in Show at Hitchin and was in the last three of the East Anglian Super Match. Latest in the line are the two puppies Janavons Cha-Cha-Cha and Janavons Bobby Dazzler. Bobby, at his first show, was third in a big Utility Puppy Group.

KERTELLAS (Black)
Roger Edward Bayliss has owed Standard Poodles since 1953. Kertellas

kennels was established in 1961. The first sire was the resoundingly well-known dog Champion Roushkas Pacific with 35 CC and 31 Res. CC. He was the sire of many Champions, his last being Champion Classic Affair at Kertellas which he sired at twelve-and-a-half years old. The first dam was Sablecomb Beyond the Fringe whose granddaughter, Champion Kertellas South Pacific, won 16 CC and was the dam of Champion Kertellas High Finance, a Spillers Dog of the Year finalist. To date there have been many Standard Poodle Champions in the UK, Scandinavia, Germany, USA, Australia and New Zealand. This kennel bred the youngest Standard Poodle ever to win a title – Ch. Kertellas Kiss and Run to Novarre.

MALIBU (Black, Brown)
Bette Sillito-Pearson started her Malibu kennel of Standard Poodles in 1958 with a cream bitch, Frenches Heather Girl from the dam Ch. Frenches Spring Heather. Then came Sylphic Dark Charmer who was to win Bette her first Best in Show at Midland Counties. Following a period of handling for the Martingdale kennel of whites from the Alekai line, Bette purchased a black bitch, Balnoble Grandma's Legacy, from Anne Beswick, from a litter sired by the import Ch. Bibelots Tall Dark and Handsome, the dam being Balnoble Legacy of a Legend. Balnoble Grandma's Legacy was later mated to Sarcell Pacemaker Romulus to produce Malibu Beach Boy of Sarcell, who is the sire of the infinitely famed Ch. Roushkas Pacific.

Meanwhile Bette's daughter Kim was making a name for herself showing the notable brown, Balnoble Bracken Tweed, one CC and 11 Res. CCs. Dawn of Olingbourne, who was owned by Audrey Bowden, had a litter sired by Vicmars Balnoble Royale, which Bette reared for Audrey, and she retained a dog which was to become Ch. Abendow Captain Cuttle. Grandma's Legacy was mated to Vulcan He's a Hobo which produced Malibu Beachmaster. Many CC-winning Standards were bred here. Margery Cleaver used Captain Cuttle on Vulcan Wicked Lady and Bette had back a black puppy which was to become Ch. Captains Lady from Malibu. This bitch also won a Best of Breed at Crufts.

Exported to Norway, Malibu Onedin and Malibu Razamataz became top producers. Their progeny were later to return to England to produce more top winners. Cross-breeding the Bracken and Legacy lines produced Ch. Malibu Light My Fire and Ch. Malibu Too Hot To Handle. Malibu then had a rest from Standards for ten years, only to return with a black bitch from Ann Rawlingson. Bette took the bitch to her title. She was Ch. Highla Indianna Hits Malibu and was joint top winning bitch in 1996. Mated to Anne Beswick's Groomar Dangerous Liaison with Balnoble produced the bitch Malibu Indysputably who was Best Puppy in Show SPC Championship Show 1996, and the brown top winning dog Ch. Malibu Indy-screet, a Group 2 winner at Southern Counties 1997.

MONTRAVIA (Black, White)
Peter and Pauline Gibbs started with their Standard Poodles in the early 1960s. They were later joined by their daughter Marita (now Marita Rogers) who won her first CC at 11 years of age. Their first Standard was the black dog, Jupiter, who won a first at the LKA. A black male from Chestal and an apricot

Ch. Montravia Royal Rumour: Top Standard Poodle of the Year 1996.

Photo: John Hartley.

from Alpenden came next. Montravia Dark and Dreamy from Marylin Willis became the first Champion. In the 1970s the black male Am. Ch. Montravia Acadia Nevermore Neville was imported and gained his English title. This dog produced black, brown, white, apricot and silver. The first blue and silver litter (by Ch. Janavons Midnight Blue) was then produced. Two imported dogs, the black Ch. Acadia Detonater, and the white Stagedoor Johnny, were significant in producing success in these two colours.

Ch. Montravia Gay Gunner took the Breed Record for CCs, with a total of 36, from his grandfather Detonater. He was also Top Standard for two years. His son, Ch. Montravia Tommy Gun, was Top Standard for the following three years, winning 53 CCs as well as attaining the accolade of Top Dog all Breeds in 1984 and Best in Show at Crufts 1985. His daughter, Ch. Star of a

Gun, became Top Standard for the follow three years, winning 48 CCs. Montravia have achieved Top Standard dog or bitch over 15 times.

Next came success when using the Spanish import Ch. Del Zarzozo Palomo at Mankia and the import from South Africa, Ch. Leander Stockbrocker of Montravia. In 1990 Don Fernando was Top Standard and Top Utility. That year Montravia won four Groups with three different Standards – Don Fernando, Stockbrocker and Donna Lisa – all within eight days. In 1994 another import, this time from America, joined Montravia and was made an English Champion in four shows, Am. Ch. Baybreeze Prince of Tides at Montravia, joint Top Standard in 1995 and Best of Breed at Crufts 1996. Mated to a Tommy Gun daughter, Guns 'n Gossip, he produced the Top winning CC Standard and the Standard Poodle Club dog of the Year for 1996, Ch. Montravia Royal Rumour. Standards in Montravia ownership have won 274 CCs.

MYALL (White, Black)
Chris and Ray Uings' first Standard came in 1970, an apricot from Tiopepi. Then came Ch. Lentella Chorus Girl from the American import Ch. Acadia Stagedoor Johnny of Leander and the dam Lentella Annie Get Your Gun. A significant dog bred by the Rev. Ford and co-owned with Miss Helen Barnes was campaigned by Chris, Ch. Davlen The Beloved, who was sired by the Spanish import Ch. Del Zarzoso Palomo at Namkia, and whose dam was Ch. Lentella Love Affair. This dog won 19 CCs and 10 Res. CCs, 15 Best of Breeds and the Utility Group at Crufts 1989. He was Top Sire in 1987 and Top Stud in 1988. Beloved has sired many top winning Standards.

Ch. Davlen The Beloved: The sire of many top winning Standards.

Ch. Malibu Beach Boy Of Sarcell.
Photo: Diane Pearce.

SARCELL (Black)
Jill Ashwick started with her first Standard in 1961, Sarcell Pacemaker Romulus. The Sarcell kennels have produced continuous winning dogs, including a Best of Breed winner at Crufts 1975, Champion Sarcell All That Jazz. Jill has owned other memorable Standards that have contributed to the quality blacks in many parts of the world including Australia, in particular through Ch. Malibu Beach Boy of Sarcell.

SHALANKA (White)
Ann Penfold started showing in the 1960s. Her first Standard Poodle was a bitch sired by Champion Bibelots Tall Dark and Handsome. Next came Abeyridge Red Apache from the Tiopepi kennels; he won two Res. CCs. Ann then purchased and took to her title the bitch Champion Heaven Sent from Tiopepi.

Following this came Champion Vicmar's Merry Hell at Shalanka. This bitch subsequently proved to be a winning brood and won Ann the title of Top Breeder 1988 and she was Top Brood bitch 1989. Champion Quiet a Riot at Vicmars, owned by Ann, was a Group winner and won Reserve Best in Show at the Scottish All Breed Championship Show. Champion Shalanka's Dancing Brave (Champion Davlen The Beloved ex Merry Hell) came next, followed by Shalanka's So Blessed, a CC and Best of Breed winner. Champion Devil in Demand at Shalanka, BOB Crufts 1988, mated to Merry, produced Champions in Finland, Russia and Germany. The imported Champion Dassin Donahue at Shalanka won Best in Shows as well as the Group at Crufts. This dog sired two Champions for Ann before leaving to live in Singapore.

Ch. Vicmars Merry Hell At Shalanka: An important brood bitch.

SUPERNOVA (Black)
Melva and Keith Nathan started their kennel in 1969. They have since achieved 11 Champions – two of which are Championship Show Group winners. Their first male was Champion Parkro Court Royal of Supernova JW. Champion Midshipman at Kertellas Supernova, sired by Ch. Roushkas Pacific won five Best In Shows at all-breed Championship Shows and nine Groups. In 1979 he was Top Utility and Pro Dog of the year and runner-up Champion dog of the year. In 1980 Midshipman was runner-up in the Contest Of Champions. He was Top Dog in the Breed 1979 and 1980. In all, he won 25 CCs. Supernova have won Dog of the Year with five different dogs. Other Champions include USA, Germany, Norway and Ireland.

TIOPEPI (Apricot)
Clare Coxall registered this kennel in 1957. The first Tiopepi Standard Poodle Champion was Ch. Tiopepi Baymer

Golden Sunrise, born in 1970, a son of Champion Alpenden Golden Sand. He won Best of Breed at Crufts in 1976. In 1980 Clare bred the apricot Champion Tiopepi Kitten of the Quays, sired by Sunrise. Clare, after judging in America and falling in love with a black puppy, purchased him, and this dog, Champion Dassin Diablo at Tiopepi, produced many Champions and winning stock; he was Top Stud Dog in 1983 and 84. Many of his children have also produced Champions. The most famous offspring from Diablo was the Crufts Best In Show winner Champion Montravia Tommy Gun, bred by Clare.

VALERITE (Silver, Blue)
Val and John Wright registered their kennel in 1974. The first dam was Alpenden Gold Melody, bred by Mrs Vivienne Kellard. This bitch won Best in Show at an Open Show, and gained a Stud Book number. The silver bitch Vulcan Champagne Starturn was

Ch. Christabelle To Valerite.

Photo: John Hartley.

purchased from the Vulcan kennels and was to become the Valerites' first Champion in 1979. She was the dam of the Canadian Champion Valerite Shine on Bibelot's, sired by Champion Janavons Midnight Blue. Champion Bluebell from Valerite came next and was subsequently the dam of probably the highest-winning silver bitch Champion, Christabelle to Valerite. This bitch won 13 Puppy classes with several Best Puppy awards, and 5 Res. CCs. She appeared in the Crufts Centenary Pageant. The latest blue to be campaigned is Valerite Got the Blues who has achieved several Best Puppy awards.

VICMARS (White, Black)
In 1975 at the age of twelve Sharon Pine-Haynes became the proud owner of Vicmars all the Rage, a daughter of Vicmars Gala Royale, sired by the legendary Ch. Vicmars Balnoble Royale. The Vicmars kennels at this time was owned by John and Vicky Marshall.

Sharon took another bitch from the Vicmars kennel and this was to become her first Champion, Vicmars in Demand, the winner of 13 CCs and two Groups, handled by Geoff Corish. A male was then purchased from Vicmars, which Sharon took to his title, Champion Vicmars Royale Show at Gaieval. He was to win 8 CCs and 16 Res. CCs. It was during the time of campaigning Royale Show that Vicky emigrated to Australia and asked Sharon to take over the reins at Vicmar. Sharon's first home-bred Champion was Ch. Vicmars Devils Disciple at Gaieval, a Crufts Best of Breed winner. Several other Champions have followed, including Vicmars Hells Angel, Angelic Upstart at Vicmars, Vicmars Aint a Saint and Vicmars Blithe Spirit; the latest is Champion Vicmars Val Hallen.

VULCAN (White, Silver, Black)
Ann Coppage came to the Vulcan kennels of the Hon. Mrs Ionides and

Ch. Vicmars Val Hallen.
                    Photo: Diane Pearce.

Neiger Silver Fox For Vulcan (imp. Australia) with his daughter Vulcan Silver Possum (exp. USA).   Photo: Diane Pearce

Shirley Walne in 1955 for a year's training as a kennel maid. She started to handle the show dogs and stayed on. Following the death of Nellie Ionides she was asked by Shirley to become a partner. Ann says she really does not know how many Champions the Vulcan kennels have bred, but at one time there were eleven living on the premises. Several breeders such as the Frenches, Beguinette, Highla and many more, purchased foundation stock from Vulcan. Imports by the kennel have also influenced black, white and silver bloodlines. Vulcan exports too have played their part in many countries including the USA, Canada, Australia, New Zealand, South Africa, Scandinavia and Europe.

Ann's first personally-bred sire was Vulcan Champagne Gold Fancy, a cream descendant of the litter sister to Ann's first personally-owned Standard Poodle, Champion Vulcan Champagne Damassin; those of us that remember her and have Vulcan Damassin offspring know she was a very special lady. 1969 was a special year for Vulcan when Vulcan Psyche of Gayshaws won the Utility Group at Crufts.

IRELAND
DONOLLIE (Black)
John and Roisin Macdougald started their kennel in 1960 with a Gaystream bitch; she was mated to Irish Ch. Courageous of Olingbourne. Ch. Vulcan Pacemaker He's a Tramp was later used on this bitch and Ch. Vulcan Champagne He's a Hobo came to live at Donollie, gaining his Irish title. Other studs including Ch. Wycliffe Ovation for Vulcan and Ch. Taiga Master Titan contributed to the success of the kennel,

which took ten Standards to their Irish title – eight home-bred. John and Roisin have bred one overseas Champion, Am. Ch. Donollie Tohah of Kissena. Recently imported is the only white in a family of blacks, now Irish Ch. and with one CC, Magnolia from Vanitonia at Donollie.

KELYN (White)
Lyn Richardson made up her first Standard in 1986, Ch. Moonlight at Mineret's and Kelyn (Ziggi). She then moved to Ireland where two daughters of Ziggi's won Green Stars. The latest arrival, Likoni Monday's Child, is a Green Star and Best in Show winner.

KISSENA (Black, White)
Rose McCabe started her kennel with a puppy from Donollie, Jonah of Kissena, a black who went to Rose in New York in 1986. The bitch was handled by Mary Shanoff to become the first Irish-bred Standard Poodle to become an American Champion. Rose returned to Ireland in 1993 and the Kissena kennels were rejuvenated with a white male, Tamoretta Pearly Spencer of Kissena – BISS Dundalk Championship Show 1986.

MARVALARCH (Black, White)
A black Standard, Vulcan Rising Star, arrived with Val and Mary Coghlan in 1975, and their affix was registered in 1980. From the late Mrs Ann Tipson, from the acclaimed Kelramo kennels, came what was to be the first dog to gain a title for Val and Mary – Irish Ch.

Ir. Ch. Magnolia From Vanitonia At Dunollie.

*Tamoretta Pearly
Spencer Of Kissena.*

Kelramo Pink Generation. The first home-bred Irish Champion, Marvalarch Vigalo, was crowned in 1986 – he was the Annual Champion. His litter mate, owned by Mr and Mrs J. Dobson, became Irish Ch. Marvalarch Temptation, who also won the Annual Championship. In 1987 came Irish Ch. Kelramo Gun Swinger, who won the Annual Championship, five Utility Groups, one Res. Best in Show and one BIS All Breed Championship Show.

1988 saw home-bred Irish Ch. Marvalarch Babylon gain a title and BIS winner. In 1992 Irish Ch. Kelramo Smooth Operator was made up. In 1996 the seventh Irish Champion came in the guise of Glynpeder Femme Fatale who, in 1995, had also gained the distinction of being the first bitch in Ireland to be awarded a CACIB under FCI rules at the 8th World Congress of Kennel Clubs International Dog Show.

11

STANDARD POODLES IN NORTH AMERICA

There has always been a warm and special relationship between the British and their American and Canadian friends. This is no less true in the world of Standard Poodles. However, dog showing on the opposite side of the Atlantic is very different in its system to the British show scene. There are many Poodle Clubs in the different States and some of them are dedicated to one colour – The Apricot/Red PC, The Silver PC.

THE POODLE CLUB OF AMERICA
Probably the most significant one is The Poodle Club of America whose National Specialty is considered to be one of the most spectacular shows for Poodles in the world. The PCA spectacular is held in a huge, air-conditioned stadium which is virtually transformed into an indoor park. The show incorporates major Poodle activities including Conformation and Obedience. The show attracts large entries, a staggering figure of 954 in 1995, though this number does include the three sizes of Poodle and the Obedience competitors. A notable aspect here is the number of overseas visitors,

who contribute to making it a truly international affair. Poodles carry bloodlines from many parts of the world, which creates a stimulating and educating cross-section of ideas between breeders, judges and those with an interest in the breed.

The Breed Standard of America was drawn up on December 10th 1885. The first Poodle Club was formed in 1886. This was later dissolved, to be re-formed in 1931. Some early breeders were recorded as the Misses Alger, Mr and Mrs Trevor, Mr Moulyon and Mr Jackson. Original founder members of the Poodle Club were Mr and Mrs Sherman Hoyt, Mrs Byron Rogers, Mr Lorning Marshal, Mr and Mrs Putman and Mr and Mrs Charles Price.

EARLY POODLE IMPORTS
Poodles were imported into North America, mostly from England, as early as the 1880s. A dog, Fecken, whelped in 1873, and another called Michael Angelo, whelped in the same year, were imported to America, and the latter won First Prize at the New York Dog Show. A Monsieur Dachateau bred the remarkable

Poodle, Styx, in 1885. This renowned dog won many prizes in England before leaving to live in America, where he won highest honours. In the 1990s the Standard Poodle became popular with several kennels who were expert in producing a good type.

However, very few Poodles were registered at the American Kennel Club around 1900. They did not share the popularity that the breed enjoyed in the UK. But there were breeders, such as the ones mentioned above, who persevered with the breed. Mr Charles Price of Boston purchased from Sir Harry Moorhouse all the best of the dogs Sir Harry had inherited from the famous Chieveley Kennel, following the death of his sister, Miss Mary Moorhouse, in 1929. Three of these dogs, Ch. Chieveley Chopstick, Ch. Chieveley Chump and Ch. Chieveley Chess, played a considerable part in producing quality miniatures in the USA.

The owner of the Nymphaea Kennel, Mrs Hutchinson, had mostly German stock which had been imported into the UK and then exported to the US. A Standard dog from this background was Ch. Nymphaea Jason, who was to sire many winning Poodles in the US. The most noted of his offspring was Ch. Blakeen Cyrano, bred by Mrs Sherman Hoyt. Cyrano's dam was Blakeen Vigee Le Brun, a daughter of Ch. Nymphaea Jason.

THE BLAKEEN KENNEL

At about the same time, Mrs Hoyt imported from England, from Mr and Mrs Harper, Ch. Harpendale Monty of Blakeen. Of some significance was the bitch Anita of Lutterspring, originally from Germany, which, when mated to Nymphaea Pice, produced, in one litter,

The legendary Int. Ch. Nunsoe Duc de la Terrasse of Blakeen.

two Champions. They were Roulette and Paul of Misty Isles. These two dogs, at the age of two months, went to Mrs Hoyt, who was to mastermind the famous Blakeen Kennel. She was a notable figure in the US and it is said of her that nobody was a better judge than she as to what really was the best. Her kennel was world-famous and produced many Champions.

In 1934 she imported the supreme white boy, Int. Ch. Nunsoe Duc de la Terrasse. This magnificent dog first came to Miss Jane Lane in England from Switzerland. He was a dog noted for his beautiful coat, his great dignity, his superior intelligence and his gentle nature. He created a lot of excitement in America and was to become a national figure. He excelled not only in beauty but also in intelligence. He was the first Standard Poodle to win Best in Show at the prestigious Westminster Show. He sired many Champions, including Ch. Blakeen Jungfrau, and Am. Can. Ch. Blakeen Eiger. He was an incredible dog and was never defeated in the Breed in America.

The Puttenstove Kennel owned by Mr and Mrs George Putman was a noted kennel that produced many Champions whose breeding goes back to Ch. Blakeen Cyrano and Ch. Harpendale Monty of Blakeen. There is more about this kennel when we are discussing the leading kennels later in the chapter.

In both America and the UK, breeders have encouraged all colours, and much interest has always been taken in producing good colour stock. As we see in the leading kennels list, top producers come from different colours. However, in the US as in the UK, the black and the white still seem to reign.

In North America Standard Poodles are more frequently handled by professional handlers who travel with their exhibits thousands of miles from show to show. Dogs from other countries are often flown into North America to gain their title or Championship, which is achieved on the points system, as stated in the chapter on Showing. There are many more shows in America than in Britain. Entries are largest at the Specialty shows run by the Poodle Clubs. Because of the importance of the influence of the US breeders in the development of the Standard Poodle, reference is made to them throughout this book, and their expertise, knowledge and friendship is treasured.

REBECCA MASON

A prominent figure in the Poodle World of North America, and President of the PCA from 1971-1974 – which, it is noted, she was personally responsible for pulling out of a low ebb to the dramatic, first-class, elegant and glamorous show it is today – was the inspirational Rebecca

Mason of the Bel Tor Poodles. She also initiated the concept of the travelling Specialty which has since become the PCA Regional. In her administration the Illustrated Standard was conceived. This well-respected lady was well known for generously giving her time and expertise to help those with a genuine interest in the breed.

Becky (1908-1996) still remains, today, best known as the top breeder of American Poodle Champions in American history. Besides breeding some 225 American Champions under the Bel Tor prefix, her stud dogs have produced very many Champions to bitches from many different kennels.

She was born with an interest in dogs, coming from a family where her father raised Champion Airedales and Wire Fox Terriers on his farm in Torrington, Connecticut. However, when she married Jess A. Mason and inherited two step-children, her new husband found he had inherited five Standard Poodles. They had a litter of puppies in their small house and it was here that Betty started the Bel Tor kennel. The name was inspired by the names of her two children from her first marriage, Belinda and Toby, and her own name.

Miss Mary McCreery of the Lowmont Kennel had a significant influence on Becky and sold her several of her dogs, including Lowmont Lady Joseph, who was to become her foundation bitch.

Her favourite bitch was Ch. Bel Tor Hosanna. She was a stud fee puppy from her dog, Lowmont Monsieur Hercule Poirot, and a Surrey bitch. Becky saw this arrogant bitch looking down her nose at her and took her home, remarking that she was the most remarkable, intelligent and sensitive dog she had ever owned. Hosanna produced nine Champions, including the top producer Ch. Bel Tor Gigadibs.

This very significant lady, Becky Mason, was described as "a wonderful example of what an energetic, educated, brilliant woman could make of her life at a time when options were much more limited for women."

TOP DOGS

A significant dog in the US in more recent years is the internationally bred dog from a combination of bloodlines, Ch. Maneetas Del Zarzoso Fuego Fatuo, alias Gordon. From the dog Sw. Norw. Ch. Harbbovi's Heaven Can Wait and the bitch Del Zarzoso Boquita Pintada, Gordon was born in England, one of twelve puppies. Juan Cabrera of the Del Zarzoso kennels said Gordon had the most extrovert temperament, was very, very exaggerated in all parts, and had promising virtues. Gordon went to Spain at eight weeks old, and was later shown twice, before leaving to accomplish an undefeated puppy career with the handlers Dennis McCoy and Randy Garren in the USA. He soon became an American Champion.

Gordon went back to Spain to win several reserves to Best in Show and Groups. His next port of call was to Finland, to Tina and Juha Palosaari. Gordon won one Best in Show after another. He finished his year in Finland as Top Dog of All Breeds ever. And then, for this well-travelled dog, it was back to the USA. The Poodle Club of America was his first show on this second time in this country. He received enormous international applause. He finished Best Standard in Show.

Gordon has been used at stud nearly a hundred times, it is claimed. Many of his children and grandchildren now grace

the rings in the USA and elsewhere. His wins top nearly 200 Group firsts, more than 50 all-breed Best in Shows, 10 Specialty Best in Shows and Number One Non-Sporting dog in America. He was Top dog in 1993. Gordon is now retired to his home in Spain.

Another significant dog in the US was the all-time top winning Poodle male, Ch. Whisperwind's On A Carousel. He was from a litter by Ch. Primetime Kristofer ex Ch. Whisperwind Brooke that also produced two other Champions, Ch. Whisperwind Free Spirit and Ch. Pinafore Pirate Whisperwind, who was No. 1 Standard in Japan. Known as Mr Personality, On A Carousel was always so full of fun, always happy with tail wagging. He finished in 1987. One weekend he won three Best in Shows and, another time, four BIS in a row. This magnificent dog won 101 BIS, 18 Specialties and 239 Group Firsts. The conclusion of his show career came with a BIS win at Westminster 1991. He was to become a top producer of his time. The Whisperwind kennel of Linda Blackie is one of the top kennels in the US.

US LEADING KENNELS

I would like to thank Elaine Robinson, Molly Windebank and Ann Penfold for helping me compile this list of US kennel names. I think we have a fair representation of good dogs here.

ASCOT (Black)

Ed and Glenna G. Carlson established their kennels in 1970. They have bred no fewer than 57 Champion Standard Poodles. They were the breeder/owners of the 1990 Best of Breed at the Poodle Club of America Show with Ch. Ascot Easy Does It, from an entry of 999 all

Am. Ch. Ascot Easy Does It

ATLANTA (Black, White)
Toni and Martin Sosnoff started their kennel in late 1987 and for many years had various Standard Poodles from the renowned Bel Tor kennels of Becky Mason. Bel Tor Glitter 'N Glo, a beautiful brown, was to be the first to produce a home litter for Atlanta. A daughter from this litter, Atlanta Do It For Becky, was the first Standard Toni and Martin finished and she went on to become a top producer. At the same time Ch. Legacy Midnight Tango was acquired; she was Winners Bitch at the Poodle Club of America in 1989. Also acquired was the bitch Ch. DeNevillette Rumor Has It who had a solid career as a Special. Both these girls are top producers and instrumental in establishing an active breeding program, producing many Champions. In 1994-95 Ch. Atlanta Alize was the number one Standard Poodle (all systems) and the number two non-sporting dog (all systems) in the United States. Alize also won the variety at the Regional Poodle Club of America 1994 as well as two awards of merit at the National. Ch. Atlanta Memory of Midnight finished

varieties. They were the breeders of Ch. Ascot On Request, Winners Dog, The Poodle Club of America 1994. They are also owners of top producers Ch. Wycliffe Nocturne, Ch. Wycliffe Xcellente of Shamlot and Ch. Wycliffe Fanfare at Ascot. They bred the top producers Ch. Ascot Anna, Ch. Ascot Emily, Ch Ascot Olivia, Ch. Ascot Patrick, Ch. Ascot Xcalibur, Ch. Ascot Easy Does It, Can. Ch. Ascot Nice 'N Naughty Vetset and Ch. Ascot On Request. Ascot Standard Poodles work in Agility and Obedience as well as the conformation ring. Although essentially black, with an occasional cream, Ascot now have their first brown after 27 years.

Am. Ch. Atlanta Alize.

Ashbey Photography.

1996 as number two Standard Poodle (Pedigree). The bitch, Ch. Atlanta Nicole, is the latest to star in Specials career.

BLUE SKIES (Black)
Patricia Moulthrop has achieved considerable success breeding just one litter a year after starting her kennel in 1980. To date 56 Champions have secured their title, owned or bred by Patty. She has also bred a German/Dutch Champion, an Australian and Indonesian Champion, and three Canadian Champions. Two of the US Champions are Multiple Best in Show and Multiple Specialty Best in Show winners; 1992 Westminster Kennel Club Group Second. Patty has an interest in Obedience and has now started to enjoy the fun of Agility. Her favourite classes are Puppy and Veteran. A win which caused immense joy was with Ch. Gorgis Blue Skies Alice B who won the Veteran Sweepstakes at the PCA National in 1993.

CALBRECHT
Sharon Calbrecht, a life-long animal lover, started her Standard Poodle kennel in 1964 with Calbrecht Sally Dubychet. Sharon learned from showing Sally that it took more than a good-quality dog to win. It takes a lot of grooming. The first quality show dog was Calbrecht's Tanya of St. Ives, mostly from Mayfield breeding. Her first breeding was to Ch. Dassin Debauchery, which produced two Champions, Ch. Calbrecht's Cordon Blue and Ch. Calbrecht's Madonna of Pride. Her second litter was sired by Ch. Mimzer the Centurian, which produced Ch. Calbrecht's Sweet Honesty. Her last litter was sired by Ch. Mecal Jerimiah which produced three Champions – Ch.

Calbrecht's Black Bart, Ch. Calbrecht's Avenging Angel and Ch. Calbrecht's Captain Courageous. Ch. Calbrecht's Ring of Fire was a favourite dog. He produced 40 Champions. One of them, Ch. Calbrecht's Jack Daniels, has sired 23 Champions. Some other outstanding dogs are Ch. OTCh. Calbrecht's Montpellier UD, Ch. Calbrecht's K-C of Mayfield, Ch. Calbrecht's Academy Award UD, Ch. Millennium Sun Sational and a favourite, Ch. Calbrecht's Rose Is A Rose, the dam of nine Champions.

CHORUS LINE
Although he recently passed away (January 1997), Bill Carter's Chorus Line kennel of Standard Poodles must be noted. A man whose character was often likened to the breed he so adored, Bill began breeding and showing under the watchful eye of Tom Carneal (Peckerwood). Although these two men lived miles apart, a beneficial arrangement between them endured for many years.

Bill was noted, during his phenomenal career, as a skilled groomer and an accomplished handler. He rarely handled dogs which were not of his own breeding. Some of his notable dogs were Ch. Chorus Line Magnum PI, Best in Variety PCA 1984, a top producer. Ch. Chorus Line Patty was one of the top winning dogs from the kennel. Ch. Chorus Line Bruce was a Best variety at PCA Regional in Chicago 1978 under the renowned Jean Lyle. Then there were Ch. Chorus Line Preston Denison, Ch. Chorus Line Mr Rigby and Ch. Peckerwood's She Promised Me, co-owned with Tom Carneal.

Bill Carter bred a total of 31 Champions, plus several Canadian and

European Champions. Ch. Chorus Line Magnum PI sired 69 American Champions and one Obedience Trail Champion as well as several foreign Champions. The most remarkable characteristic he passed to his offspring, along with elegance and style, was a beautiful temperament. Probably one of the most charming epitaphs I ever read was to Magnum: "He was a gentleman, who left the impression that he was a 17th Century Cavalier, bowing to his many girlfriends before and after breeding them, and perhaps leaving a love poem pinned to their pillow."

DASSIN
Freeman 'Bud' Dickey and Joseph Vergnetti experienced phenomenal success from the late 1960s. Dassin dogs of reputation are Ch. Jocelyene Marjorie, Ch. Dassin Blue Tango O'Charmer, Ch. Dassin Debauchery, Ch. Dassin's Sum Buddy, Ch. Dassin Sashtie, Ch. Dassin Debussy, Ch. Dassin Rita La Rose, Ch. Dassin Delux, Ch. Dassin Stella Dora and Ch. Dassin Marjarita.

Bud first got into dogs when he was a kid of about 14. The first dog he was to own was a Cocker Spaniel. He was dating a girl who had Beagles; her best friend had a white Miniature Poodle. Bud took the little Poodle to a match in conformation, went Best in Match – and that was it. He was hooked, and hooked on Poodles. Joseph Vergnetti, the long-term partner of the Dassin Kennels, has continued his handling career since the death of Bud in 1994.

DeNEVILLETTE
Connie Rogers saw a Standard Poodle in the paper for $50 – and thus Jenny came into her life. The next Poodle was purchased in 1975 and became Ch.

DeNevillette Eclipse. Her adult size was 27 inches and her weight around 85 pounds. The bitch, from Wendall Sammet, who later became Ch. Alekai DeNevillette Wahine, was the second foundation bitch. The third, in 1980, was to become Ch. Torchlight Mia DeNevillette. The first breeding was Ch. DeNevillette Eclipse to Ch. Wycliff Xcellente of Shamlot. From this came Ch. DeNevillette Sweet Emotions, who finished with four majors from bred-by classes. The second breeding was the Alekai bitch to Ch. Gervais Tabu which produced Ch. DeNevellitte Dapper Dan, a top producer. Their breeding was by Dapper Dan to Mia, which produced Can. Ch. DeNevillette Dea of Gilvi and from Dea came two Champion males.

DONNCHADA (Black, White, Cream)
This is the affix of Elizabeth (Betty) Brown and Barbara Leonard. Betty started the Donnchada line in 1973. Barbara became one of Betty's clients in 1987 and they became partners in 1990. They have produced 60 AKC Champions. Nestled in seven acres in Spring, Texas is the Victorian home where several top dogs have been produced. Betty is currently showing Multiple Best in Show Ch. King's Champagne Taste, who is totally out of the Donnchada line. In 1995/6 he was one of the top five Standards in the USA. Ch. Donnchada Candybear and her daughter Ch. Donnchada Allure Affirmed have won Best Brood Bitch at the PCA Nationals. Betty and Barbara have been working on a silver line for the last four years and feel they are achieving success with a line equal to their black, white and cream lines. Health testing is a priority at the kennels, which currently have five top producers. Betty gave

Barbara Candybear in 1987; she finished her Championship with a 5 point major during the National Specialty weekend in St Louis, Mo. She has several BIS and has twice won Best Brood Bitch in National Shows. Candy has produced 10 Champions. For the past four years Donnchada have consistently been one of the top three producers of AKC Champions in the USA.

GRAPHIC

Florence Graham started with her Standard Poodles in 1960 competing in Obedience, then Utility Degree. She is an owner/breeder and exhibitor with 40-plus Champions to her credit. A personal best was WB and BOW at PCA, WD at PCA from the Bred-by Exhibitor class, with litter mates who were just one year old, Ch. Graphic Helvetica and Ch. Graphic Bodoni Extra Bold. Ch. Graphic Good Fortune sired PCA Best of Variety winner Ch. Ascot Easy Does It. Other notable dogs are Ch. Graphic Constellation, WM at PCA; co-bred Ch. Bluebell Audacious, WB at the PCA Regional; and Ch. Graphic Copperplate Gothic sired Best Puppy at PCA Regional. Good Fortune has an Obedience Trail Champion and his brother sired a sled dog racing in a team in Alaska. Graphic Double Take went on from being a stunning puppy to win World Show in Copenhagen. A Good Fortune daughter, Savarin Cold Cold Heart, is the product of frozen semen imported to Australia.

LEMERLE (Blue, Silver, White, Black)

Dr Elaine Robinson started breeding Standard Poodles over 20 years ago while living in Brisbane, Australia. To date (1996) she has bred, shown and/or owned two black Australian Champions,

Am. Can. Ch. Lemerle Lite My Fire.
Photo: Dave Ashbey.

33 black American Champions, five white American Champions, three blue American Champions, two silver American Champions and numerous Canadian Champions as well as Obedience Champions. Lemerle Standard Poodles have been exported to Canada, England, Brazil, Germany, Denmark, Finland and South Africa. Elaine has imported four English Standard Poodles since 1985, including Ch. Larling Sweet Liberty at Kertellas and Am. Can. Ch. Kertellas Blatant Lie At Lemerle, winner of Best Stud Dog at the Poodle Club of America National Specialty in 1996. The white bitch, Am. Can. Ch. Lemerle Lite My Fire was Best Standard Puppy and Reserve Winners Bitch at the Poodle Club of America National Specialty Show in 1991, and subsequently became a multiple Best in Show winner in Canada. Elaine bred the top-winning silver Standard Poodle of all time, Am. Can. Ch. Lemerle French Silk, winner of 12 All-Breed Best in Shows,

Am. Can. Ch. Nevermore Jordan.

Best of Variety at the PCA National Specialty in June 1995, seven Poodle Specialty Best in Shows, and Awards of Merit at PCA and Westminster Kennel Club shows.

NEVERMORE (Black)
Sue Henley started her kennel in 1960 and has, since then, bred 34 litters, producing 41 American and Canadian Champions, Multiple Group, Best in Show, and Best in Specialty Show winners. The majority of these winners were breeder-owner handled. Sue bred the Show Dog of the Year 1994. Three of her dogs have Companion Dog degrees, two have Tracking Dog degrees, Tracking Dog Excellent, eight have Canine Good Citizen awards, ten are Certified Therapy Dogs, and she has had seven Poodle Club of America Top Producers. Sue was elected to the Poodle Club of America Board of Directors as the Standard Poodle Representative for

two years. She was Breeder of the Year at the Gig Harbor Kennel Club; she received the Inspirational Award from the Puget Sound Poodle Club and the Award for Outstanding Contribution and Dedication to the World of Dogs from the Seattle Kennel Club and is President of the Puget Sound Poodle Club, and of Gig Harbor Kennel Club. Currently she is a member of the Northwest Poodle Obedience Club, and the Rainier Agility Team.

PINAFORE
Penny Harney started with her Poodles in 1962. Her first was a miniature from the famous Puttoncove Kennel. She began competing at AKC shows for Obedience and then got fascinated with the Poodle coat. The first Standard was

Puttencove Day Lily CD, from which Penny bred her first Champion, Ch. Pinafore Panda Bear CD. Here was a Group winner which got Penny hooked on Conformation showing. Because the care of the coat took up so much time, Penny gave up on her Obedience to concentrate on conformation. Breeding in the Alekia line produced good results and the next Champion was Ch. Pinafore Pinocchio, also out of Day Lily.

The line includes black, white and silver and over the years has produced 80 Champions and many Best in Shows, and most are top producers. Ch. Pinafore President was the top sire, having produced over 30 Champions. Penny is also the co-breeder of the 1991 BIS Westminster winner, Ch. Whisperwind On A Carousel, whose dam was Ch.

Am. Ch. Safari's Shamus.

Pinafore Whisperwind Brooke. The latest dog, Ch. Pinafore Prestidigation, is an American, German and Swedish Champion.

SAFARI (White)

Cynthia and Mary K. Huff first became interested in Standard Poodles around 1963 when Mary was impressed by a Standard she saw at an Obedience class carrying its owner's purse in its mouth. Mary was impressed by the intelligence of the breed and purchased her first Standard, Ann, in 1964. They bred their first litter in 1971, line breeding from old Puttencove stock, a foundation which was the start of a long friendship with Mrs George Putnam. Since this beginning Safari have bred 56 Champions, mostly in America, but also in Canada, Mexico, the Netherlands, Germany and Greece and CACIB holders. In August of 1987 the Am. Can. Ch. Safari's Evensong became the top producing dam in the history of American poodles (all varieties), breaking the twenty-seven year reign held by Am. Can. Ch. Wycliffe Jacqueline, Ch. Jocelyene Marjorie, and Mollie Brown's Creme de Cacao. Two Safari dogs have won Best in Show awards at Poodle Specialties in Europe; one sired another BIS Specialty winner. Another Safari dog went BIS at the Athens International Show in 1995. Many bitches and several dogs from this kennel have qualified for top producing status from the Poodle Club of America. Unusually for the USA, most of the Champions here have been owner/breeder-handled. Three dogs in

the top twenty in the US were also owner/breeder-handled. Many Safari dogs have worked as duck dogs in the field, have served as therapy dogs and have excelled in the Obedience ring. One is also a successful 'seeing eye dog' in the US.

TORCHLIGHT (Black, Cream)

This kennel is owned by Jean Lazarus and Marcy Bernstein, and is devoted to Standard Poodles. It has been registered continuously with the AKC since 1925! Dr C. Young, a bacteriologist associated with the State Health Department in Michigan, had an interest in showing and breeding Standard Poodles. He had a place on Torch Lake, and wished to use the kennel name of Torch Lake, but this was objected to by the AKC so Torchlight emerged. Two bitches were imported from England; the first became American Champion Nunsoe Little Audrey of Torchlight, a black bitch sired by Ch. Vulcan Champagne Pommery ex Eng. Ch. Nunsoe Brown Bess. The second imported bitch was also black,

Am. Ch. Torchlight Tennyson.

Vulcan Cherry Pie of Torchlight, sired by Nunsoe Onyx out of Vulcan Verena.

Dr Young bred and showed successfully until his death in 1949, producing a number of Champions. One of his protégés at the Health Department was a bacteriologist named Frances Angela, who also had an interest in the breed. After the death of Dr Young, Fran Angela took over Torchlight, breeding and showing successfully and finishing more Champions in black, brown, cream and apricot. Jean Larazus began working with Fran Angela in the early 1960s. They co-owned the dogs but Jean raised most of the litters at her home in Wisconsin. Their last jointly-owned bitch, before Fran Angela's death, was Ch. Torchlight Derling Whervish. The bitch produced six Champions, one of whom was Ch. Torchlight Mitzvah, the dam of Ch. Aliyah Desperado, one of the top producing males in the variety in the Unites States. It is believed he had 49 Champions in all. A daughter, kept by Jean, is Torchlight Tenacious who is a top producer.

Jean inherited the Kennel and prefix and moved it to Wisconsin where it remains today. Although she originally bred apricots, Jean felt they would never achieve the quality of some of the other colours, so she changed to black, with some brown and creams. She had not any particular interest in browns, although they came along in her breeding programme regularly. They were sold to other people to show and to breed.

In 1988 Jean was joined in the kennel by Marcy Bernstein Lichtig. The joint venture provides two heads to make decisions and two homes in which to house the Poodles. They compete primarily in breed competition but have participated successfully in Obedience. An interesting event in the history of the kennel is that Torchlight Guy Tabarie CD was donated to the war effort by Fran Angela in the early 1940s. He served throughout the war as a message-carrying dog, and returned after the war. Today, Jean still holds the papers releasing him from military service and returning him to civilian life.

WESSEX (Black, White)
Charlotte and Vicky Holloway started with their Standards in 1981 with the foundation bitch Ch. Eaton Ngorongora (Ch. Longleat Alimar Raisin Cane ex Ch. Eaton Bustin With Joy). Nora produced six American Champions including Ch. Wessex Celebration who was to become one of the leading sires of all time. Since its evolution, this kennel has produced or owned numerous top producers in the USA although their breeding program has been very limited. So far 25 American Champions have been bred. In addition, Wessex has bred or owned four top ten Standards: Ch. Wessex Celebration, Ch. Wessex Kacey, Ch. Wessex Kachina Doll and Ch. Wessex Ringleader. The current brood bitch is Ch. Wessex Escapade, who was reserve Winners Bitch at the Poodle Club of America (owner-handled), with eight American Champions and with four nearly to their titles. Ch. Wessex Celebration is the only Standard sire to produce Winners Bitch at the National Specialty two years running.

LEADING KENNELS IN CANADA
BIBELOT (Silver)
This kennel is owned by Susan and Donald Fraser. Susan has owned Standard Poodles since she was a youngster. She sent the world-famous

*Am. Can. Ch.
Wycliffe Michael.*

*Photo: Linda
Lindt.*

Champion Bibelot's Tall Dark and Handsome to England to be shown and is still amazed at his wonderful success (see Chapter 1). Following TDH, who lived to be over fourteen years old, she sent a white dog to Holland who became Dutch Germ. Lux. World FCI Int. Am. Can. Ch. Bibelot's Clean as a Whistle Am. Can. CD. It was while 'Ludo' was in Holland that Susan became hooked on silvers – a colour she had been interested in since the 1950s. The first silver Champion for this kennel was Bibelot's Prosperity in Silver Am. Can. CD. Then came Am. Can. Ch. Bibelot's Signature in Silver, and more recently Am. Can. Ch. Bibelot's Lights Camera Gretion Am. Can. CD.

WYCLIFFE (Black)
Specialising in the Black colour, Jean Lyle started her breeding programe in 1952 with Wycliffe Jacqueline. Since then Jean has bred 1500 Standard Poodles of which 260 are Champions. Although mostly American and Canadian Champions, there have also been Wycliffe Champions in Europe and one in Britain. The last male Jean kept for herself was the leading sire US Can. Ch. Wycliffe Michael. The Wycliffe affix appears somewhere in the pedigrees of many of the top winning dogs throughout the world.

12 STANDARD POODLES WORLDWIDE

The Standard Poodle can truly be classed as a dog of the World. In England they have been imported from America, Canada, Spain, Scandinavia. In Australia and New Zealand the Standard Poodle is imported from England, America, Scandinavia. In Finland and Sweden American dogs have come from England and they, or their offspring, have settled in South Africa, Germany, Scandinavia, Australia, New Zealand. Standard Poodles come from South Africa to England to America, sometimes being mated and going home to have their litters.

In many parts of the world Standard Poodles are involved in so many different quarters that it is difficult to include them all. We have working Champions, we have Show Champions, we have Shooting dogs, Hunting dogs, Sled dogs, Guide dogs for the Blind, therapy dogs and others. Here are some of the leading kennels throughout the world and some of their achievements.

AUSTRALIA

AULTON (Black, White)
This kennel is owned by Cherry and Greg Glerum. Cherry started her show career at nine years old, handling for her mother. In 1981 she purchased her first Standard Poodle, Ch. Gwraggedd Moonraker, a white male. Raker won 14 placements and four in-show placements. The next Standard came in the form of Ch. Kibran Rich and Famous. Ch. Gaylea Shower O'Stars, a white bitch, was bought in; she became the top winning bitch in Victoria for the years 1993, 94 and 95, also winning a total of 34 Group placements and 16 in-show awards. Titled at just over nine months of age, she was a finalist in the Australian Day Supreme Dog Quest and also won Bitch Challenge, Best of Breed and runner-up in Group 7 at the largest dog show in the Southern Pacific, the Royal Melbourne Show, which attracted over 4500 entries in 1994.

From her first litter five white puppies were born and one black. One went to Hawaii. Another went interstate – Ch. Aulton Breathtaking I Am, which is still being shown in South Australia, with many Group Awards and in-show awards to her credit. The black bitch from this litter, Ch. Aulton Midnight N'Jamaka, was titled at just over 10 months. At six

months she won Best of Breed at the Talk to the Animals prestigious All Breeds Championship Show and Puppy in Group 7. American import Graphic Delroy Patriot has been used as stud, as has Ch. Graphic American Dream (imp. USA).

CHATAIN (Black)
Lynne and Rob Aitken have been involved with Standards since 1977, during which time they have bred 50 Champions, breeding perhaps every two years or so. Dogs from this kennel have been exported to the USA, Sweden and New Zealand. Aust. Ch. Chatain The Bitch Is Back, is a multiple All Breeds BIS winner and was BIS at the Poodle Club of Victoria. Aust. Ch. Chatain

Would I Lie to You, is also a Multiple All Breeds BIS winner. Aust. Ch. Harbovis Behind the Mask (imp. Sweden) is a Specialty CC winner at the Poodle Club of NSW and Multiple All Breeds BIS winner, and a top producer with 13 Champion children to his credit. The new baby in the ring is Chatain Feeling Hot Hot Hot, co-owned with Bob and Allison Cameron.

LOVERSLANE (Black, White)
Frank and Mary Williams (Australia) and Alan and Kerry Shrimton (New Zealand) are not big breeders, but their partnership between the two countries has produced one of the most successful show and agility kennels. Importing their first Standard Poodle from England in

165

*Aust. Ch. Chatain Would I Lie To You:
Multiple All Breeds BIS winner.*

*Aust. Ch. Loverslane The Dream CD:
BIS winner.*

1975, this combination kennel has produced notable winning stock. The bitch Aust. NZ Ch. Shaleander Dreamtime CDX HDX a top dog in her zone for two years, is the dam of Aust. Ch. Loverslane Daddy Cool, multi-Group winner. She is owned by Eve Flood, and goes for walks accompanying Eve who is in her wheelchair. Loverslane Trailblazer CDX, owned by M. Mams, is the Trial winner. Aust. Ch. Loverslane Local Hero CD, owned by Dr.D. Tudge, is the winner of three Groups. Aust. Ch. Loverslane The Dream CD is a Best in Show winner, including Poodle Specialty. NZ Ch. Loverslane Snow in Summer ADX in the course of eight shows won seven CCs, one Res. CC, and was Runner-up in Group.

NORTHLEA
Ian and Jenni Staniforth compete in Obedience, Agility, Tracking and Conformation. Their latest Standard, Aust. Ch. Chezvistra Undacova Girl UD,

TD, AD, ET, was bred by the Vieiras.
LINDA JOHNSON
She owns and trains Standards in Agility and Conformation. Aust. Ch. Neiger Circus Rose CDX, bred by N. and G. Robertson, is Multiple highest score trial winner, highest scoring Poodle at Melbourne Royale Show 1996 and a member of the Pal Super Dog Obedience, Agility and Flyball Demonstration Team. Not just a clever girl, she is also multiple Best of Breed winner in the Conformation ring. Other top dogs include Von Silbertal Narayan UD, bred by E. Zimmerman, who is Multiple Highest score on Obedience trial winner, Obedience Dog of the year 1995-96 and a member of Pal Superdog Obedience, Agility and Flyball Demonstration Team.

PAVOTS AND BALVALOR (Black)
Judy McMahon first owned the breed in the 1960s. Her first litter followed in early 1970. This kennel has bred or

NZ Ch. Loverslane Snow In Summer ADX (imp. Australia).

Aust. Ch. Sierra Solitaire Of Auro Farm: BIS winner and sire of 17 titled offspring in Australia.

owned 10 titled Standards and several Top Producers, including the American dog Ch. Sierra Solitaire of Auro Farm, jointly imported to Australia and shown by Marechal kennels. This dog has 17 titled progeny. Aust. Ch. Balvalor Body Language, a Group and Best in Show winner bred by Judy, was exported to the USA. His littermate, Balvalor Moonstruck is CDX TD, working towards TDX UD and her Australian title.

NEW ZEALAND

COSALTA (Black)

Betty and Gordon Armstrong started this kennel in 1974 with an imported dog from Australia, Ch. Pindalee Showman, who won 15 Best in Shows All Breeds and many specialist shows. Then came the English import Vicmars Royale Progress, who was sired by Ch. Rouskas Pacific. This dog produced many show winners for Cosalta including Champions. Next to come from England was the six-year-old Ch. Vicmars Razzle Dazzle, who won a Best in Show at her first show. Then came NZ Ch. Keleramo The Sinner, imported from the UK. Champion Spirit of Affirmed, bred from two American dogs, has proved a success in the breeding programme; he has won many Best in Shows in New Zealand. The latest import to this kennel is Vulcan Champagne Barrister. A great achievement for this kennel is having had four Standards pass through the Guide Dog Foundation to become Guide Dogs for the Blind.

WILDWIND (White)

This kennel started in 1973 with a dog imported from Australia from the Pindale kennels, which are founded on the Leander and Vicmars lines. The first

NZ Ch. Spirit Of Affirmed: Bred from two American dogs.

dog for Wildwind was Arkaba Garfunkel, a dog descended from Wycliffe and Vicmars. In 1982 an English dog from the American Dassin line was imported. Two Australian Royal Winners and an American Champion were produced from this line. The bitch Aust. NZ Grand Ch. Wildwind Winter Song was shown nine times in Australia, with eight Best in Shows. Grand Champion Wildwind Ice Man is top winning Standard Poodle of all time in New Zealand with over thirty Best in Shows. In all, twenty-seven Champions have been bred from this kennel.

SOUTH AFRICA

In this country, although there are only a handful of dedicated breeders, most of the world's top lines have been imported, bringing with them a high standard of quality. Most shows have, on average, about eight to ten Standards, although it has been known for an entry of 30 to be seen.

STONECOURT (Black)

Di Thompson started in 1979 with a bitch bred by the Browning sisters, Ch. Braganza Bebe Grande, from the English Torpaz line. Imported from Cambray Coppage in England came Vulcan Champagne Augustine from the American Wycliffe lines. Used on Ch. Hot Gossip at Stonecourt, the successful Ch. Stonecourt Shot in the Dark was produced. He was South Africa's top winning Standard of all time. He won six all breed Best in Shows and was Dog of the Year 1992. This dog retired at three years old having won all the major competitions. His litter sister is a Group winner and Res. Best in Show. Di also works in Obedience and working trials with considerable success.

HILLSWICK (Black, Cream)

Graham Thompson acquired his first two Standards in 1972, a black dog, Ch. Silvettas Superstar, from the Bibelot line, and the foundation bitch Ch. Chanfields Springett Milady Fayre. These two dogs gained their titles and then produced Ch. Hillswick High Handsom and his sister, Hit Number. High Handsom won seven all breed Best in Shows and 22 Groups, plus many Res BIS. Hit Number bred on for the Braganza Kennels of the Browning sisters and produced the bitch Bebe Grande, the foundation bitch for Stonecourt.

GERMANY

Breeders in Germany must abide by the stringent rules laid down by the Poodle Club. Some of these rules are:
1) Size limit for males, 62 centimeters. Bitches, 60 centimeters. Dogs which are bigger get no allowance for breeding.
2) Eyes must be checked for PRA, and

Ch. Warwick Black Yarabelle: Multi Ch. and Best in Show Champion.

Starting her breeding in 1979, Michaela has bred 50 Champions and some Best in Show winners, including Junior Champion, BIS winner Warwick White Delemma and Ch. Warwick Black Yarabelle, Multiple Champion and Best in Show Champion.

NORWAY

BRAVA (Black)
Inger Hanson purchased her first Standard Poodle in 1977, a bitch from the Malibu, Bibelot, Vulcan lines called Topsy, who achieved the title of Norwegian, Swedish and Finnish Champion. She was a fine producer who is behind all this kennel's breeding. Inger has bred 38 Standards since starting her breeding program in 1983. 14 of these have achieved Champion status. The well-known Int. Nord. Ch. Bravas Mico Superstar is on the pedigree of Standards in many different European countries. Another achiever with good Obedience results is Bravas Charff Charmer Player.

SHARP DRESSED (Black, White)
This kennel, owned by Barbara Johansson and Tom Engebretson, started in 1987 and has so far produced eight Champions – Ch. Sharp Dressed Lloyd from an English-bred sire (Ch. Supernova Stormy Impact); Ch. Sharp Dressed Scarlet O'Hara; Ch. Sharp Dressed Isadora; Ch. Sharp Dressed Alexander, Best in Show Herrenberg 91, Best in Show Baden Baden 92, Weltjugendsieger 91, Bundesjugendsieger 91, Luxemburger Jugend Ch. 91. Ch. Sharp Dressed Stormy Choice was third on the list of best Standard Poodles in Norway 1994.

knees and hips must also be checked. Only dogs with perfect hips can be bred from.
3) The size difference does not allow for more than 4 centimeters between male and female.
4) A Standard Poodle can miss three teeth, but only one Pre-molar – P1 or P2; if they miss P3 or P4 they have no allowance for breeding.
5) It is allowed only to mix black and white, or black and brown, but nothing more. If you have a poodle in the black colour, and one of its parents is white, you can only breed this black dog with a white one.

WARWICK (Black and White)
Michaela Jesionek-Hemmersbach has had a lot of success in the show ring.

Int. Nord. Ch. Bravas Micro Superstar: An influential sire.

SWEDEN
It is impossible to say when Poodles first arrived in Sweden. The Swedish Kennel Club was founded in 1891 and held a show that year in Gothenburg where Poodles were exhibited. Prior to this a few Poodles had been exhibited at the first-ever dog show in Stockholm in 1886. At the beginning of the new century Sweden had several dedicated breeders of Standard Poodles. Officially, the Swedish Poodle Club dates from 1942 (it had been preceded by a Poodle association that started five years earlier, in 1937).

AVATAR (Black, White)
This kennel was registered in 1985 by Anders Rossell. However, Anders' show career began in in the mid-70s at the age of fourteen as a groomer, and handler. The first litter was co-bred with the Davinas kennel and born in 1986. A litter is born in the Avatar kennnels every three to four years. The kennel's foundation bitch was Ch. Domestic Dark Diva Divina (Ch. Tikatee Tam O'Shanter ex Ch. Ebony Eve Ebony Charm) Licenced Rescue Dog. Ch. Avatar Davinas Dress Parade came next; she was Top Standard Bitch in Denmark in 1988, 89, 90, 91 and 92 and a Multi BIS-winner as a veteran, a multiple CC winner in Denmark and Poland and BIS-winner in Germany. Ch. Avatar Davinas

ABOVE: Ch. Sharp Dressed Scarlet O' Hara.

RIGHT: Swed. Ch. Avatar Arabica: Top winning bitch in Sweden in 1993 and 1994.

Dream On was runner-up to Top Standard in Sweden 1988 and an Obedience Trial Champion and BIS winner. Ch. Avatar Arabica came next, a top winning bitch in Sweden in 1993 and 94. Ch. Avatar Biscaya was a top winning bitch in 1995, 96; her litter brother Ch. Avatar Brazier is Danish champion and CC winner in Germany and Poland. Ch. Avatar Davinas Pandorah Froath proved her worth by producing many Champions and top-winning daughters who were among the top few in Sweden 1994. (She was a granddaughter of Champion Janavons Yankee Doodle Dandy.)

DANDY-LION (Brown)
Whenever brown Standard Poodles are mentioned in Scandinavia the Dandy-Lion prefix of Margareta and Kristina

Sahlstrom comes to mind. The first Standard bought by this mother and daughter team was a brown in 1964, who later became International and Nordic Champion. With high-quality browns being scarce in Sweden in the 1970s, Margareta and Kristina purchased some puppies from Carol Flatt's Tragapanz line and my Janavons. A brown bitch born in 1976 out of Ch. Josato Capability Brown of Tragapanz became Swedish Ch. Tragapanz Maid to Measure, and she became one of the two foundation bitches of Dandy-Lion. The other was a perky Norwegian girl, Chocolate Dream, born in 1977, a granddaughter to Ch. Malibu Onedin Line and Ch. Leander Midnight Cowboy, two imported dogs that were of great importance to the Standard Poodle breeding in Scandinavia.

*Dandy-Lion's
Blame The
Bossanova*

Very few breeders took an interest in browns in those days as they were considered difficult, with a tendency for the colour to fade. However, Dandy-Lions finished eight brown Champions and had ten additional brown certificate winners, a record according to the Swedish Kennel Club. Dandy-Lions are also very successful in blacks and, more recently, in apricots. Maid to Measure had several Champion daughters, among them Ch. Dandy-Lion's To A Wild Rose, Top Winning Black Bitch 1983. She was also the dam of Ch. Dandy-Lion's Ain't Misbehavin', a brown bitch sired by Am. Int. Nord. Ch. Eaton Kingsdown (a son to Ch. Eaton Affirmed) and Top Winning brown Standard Poodle for several years.

By Int. Nord. UK Ch. Racketeer Play It Again Sam, Chocolate Dream produced the very important black bitch Dandy-Lion's I'm Going Bananas, born in 1984, a BIS Winner. More than any other bitch, she has put her stamp on the present-day Dandy-Lion Poodles. She produced Champions and Certificate winners in every litter, including the black BIS Winner Int. Ch. Dandy-Lion's In Orbit and Ch. Dandy-Lion's Dressed For Success. Towards the end of the 1980s Dandy-Lions imported a brown male, Graphic Ambassador Teller, from Florence Graham, USA, for the benefit of a new gene-pool for Swedish and Norwegian breeders.

CARO-LINE'S (Black)
Gerty Stefenburg-Nordenstrom started her kennel in 1975. Her very first litter came in 1978. The first bitch, Int. Nord. Ch. Caroline was sired by Int. Nord. UK Ch. Racketeer Play It Again Sam (from his first litter). This bitch has produced several successful dogs. Another bitch whose progeny has proved outstanding is Sw. Nord. Ch. Ci-De-Lott's Erica For Caroline. Out of 15 puppies that this bitch produced, nine are Champions. One son of Erica's went to the Flat Hills

Fr. Swed. Ch. Cra-Line's Charismatic Cary.

Swed. Ch. Nexus Extremely Busy.

kennels in Holland and became the top winning dog there. Ch. Caro-Line's Cheerful Champ is the father of a top winning bitch as well as other Champions. He was sired by Ch. Ebony-Eve Super Shanter. Ch. Caro-Line's Captivating Cassia has had two litters with Ch. Bravas Micro Superstar, and one male from them is in Holland with the kennel of Flat-Hills; multi-Champion Caro-Line's Caring Cashet is top winning dog in Holland. Caro-Line's Charismatic Cary is in France and is French and Swedish Champion. His sister, Ch. Caro-Line's Charismatic Carrie, is the top winning bitch in Sweden 1996. Gerty has bred 20 litters with 99 puppies, of which 24 are Champions.

NEXUS (Black)
This kennel started in 1985 when Roland

and Susanne Jern-Faith bought their first Standard Poodle. They now have six Champions produced from no more than one litter a year – Ch. Nexus Wilful Wog, Ch. Nexus Extremely Busy, Ch. Nexus Busy Exhibit, Ch. Nexus Busy Example, Ch. Nexus Expressly Busy and Ch. Nexus Magic Melvin. In 1992 Wilful Wog was Top Standard Poodle in Sweden, a great achievement as this was a dog from the first litter born at Nexus. In 1993 Extremely Busy was third, and his sister Busy Exhibit was fourth on the top Standard poodle ratings. 1994 gave Busy Exhibit third rating on the top chart and best black bitch. Magic Melvin is one of the top males in Sweden 1996.

DENMARK
JOUET (Black, White)
Lena and Connie Jakobsen, a mother

Dan. VDH Ch. BDsg 96, DPKsg 96 Jouet In Spectacular Mission.

and daughter team, have been breeding Standard Poodles for the past 21 years, starting with the black foundation bitch Dan. Fr. Belg. Ger. Int. Ch. WV74 Eminent Jou-Jou Noir. This successful kennel is the current holder of 36 Champions. They have 94 Champion titles in all and are one of the leading kennels in Denmark. Bloodlines are based on stock from Denmark (Eminent), Canada (Pamela, Sanvar, Ellery, Bibelots), USA (Ledjen) and Sweden (Azadi). Puppies from this kennel have been sold all over the world as show, family and Obedience dogs.

Top dogs at the moment are the four black litter brothers and sisters (Dan. Ger. VDH Ch. Ellery The Prime Mover ex Dan. Ger. VDH Int. Ch. Jouet Joliette De Chaperon), Fr. Lux. Lj. Ch. Euuw 96, Eujsg 96, Bjsg, 6 multi BIG and BIS runner up Jouet Qualite De Joliette; Vvj 96, Ger. VDH Lj, DPKj Ch. Jouet Querelle De Joiette; Slj. Ch. Multi BIG winner Jouet Quirite De Joliette and BIS runner-up Jouet Question De Joiette.

Black sisters (Dan. Ger. VDH Ch. Jouet Shining New Hallmark ex Dan. Ger. VDH Int. Ch. Jouet Jasmine De Chaperon, litter sister to Ch. Jouet Joliette De Chaperon) are Dan. Swe. DPKj. Ch. Euw. 95, BIS and multi-winner Jouet Plaisir De Jasmine and Dan. Lux. DPKj. Ch. BOG runner-up, Jouet Politesse De Jasmine.

The litter brother and sister (Dan. Swe. Ger. Ch. DPKsg, BIS winner Jouet The Prime Sparkler ex Dan. Ch. Haerbovi Spectacular Miss), are Dan. VDH. Ch. Bdsg. 96, DPKsg 96, multi BIG and BIS runner-up Jouet In

Dan. Fr. Belg. Ger. Int. Ch. WV74 Eminent Jou-Jou Noir.

Spectacular Mission and Dan. VDH. Ger. Ch. BIS winner Jouet Doing it The Spectacular Way. A black female (Dan. Ch. Jouet Noble Made Footsteps ex Dan. Swe. Ch. BIS winner Azadi Telling Tails) is PZVj. DPKj. Ch. ABDsg 96 BIS runner-up Jouet Always On My Mind. Lena and Connie are mentors and teachers of the Crufts winner at the International Junior Handler Final 1996.